SCHOOL OF
ORIENTAL AND AFRICAN STUDIES
UNIVERSITY OF LONDON

London Oriental Series
Volume 16

LONDON ORIENTAL SERIES · VOLUME 16

NESHRĪ'S HISTORY OF THE OTTOMANS

THE SOURCES AND DEVELOPMENT OF THE TEXT

BY

V. L. MÉNAGE

Lecturer in Turkish
School of Oriental and
African Studies

LONDON
OXFORD UNIVERSITY PRESS
NEW YORK TORONTO
1964

Oxford University Press, Amen House, London E.C.4
GLASGOW NEW YORK TORONTO MELBOURNE WELLINGTON
BOMBAY CALCUTTA MADRAS KARACHI LAHORE DACCA
CAPE TOWN SALISBURY NAIROBI IBADAN ACCRA
KUALA LUMPUR HONG KONG

PRINTED IN GREAT BRITAIN

PREFACE

In a thesis accepted by the University of London for the degree of Doctor of Philosophy in 1961 I examined the interdependence of the fifteenth-century Ottoman historical works and attempted to trace the lines along which the literary traditions were transmitted. The subject necessarily entailed a careful study of the text of Neshrī, and this monograph represents the substance of various *pièces justificatives* extracted from the thesis and expanded with more liberal quotation and illustration than was feasible in the earlier context. My research was carried out under the supervision of Professor Paul Wittek, who then and since has been unstinting of his time and advice. Without attempting to expatiate on my sense of obligation to him, I ask him to accept these pages as an inadequate but sincere tribute of gratitude on the occasion of his seventieth birthday.

My thanks are due also to the authorities of the Libraries Directorate of the Turkish Republic and of the Bibliothèque Nationale, to Bodley's Librarian, and to the honorary librarian of the Chester Beatty Library for supplying me with photographic reproductions of various texts in their care.

The generosity of the Governors and the Director of the School of Oriental and African Studies enabled me to spend the session 1958–9 on study leave in Turkey, working in the public libraries of Istanbul, Ankara, and the provinces. While it would be invidious for me to single out for especial acknowledgement any of the librarians, who were uniformly helpful and patient, I cannot omit to express my indebtedness to Professor Halil Inalcık, not merely for his kind hospitality at Ankara but for the valuable conversations I have had with him on many subjects, that treated here among them.

To the School I am further indebted for the generous decision to include this work in the London Oriental Series and to bear the cost of publication.

V. L. M.

CONTENTS

BIBLIOGRAPHY

I. TEXTS OF NESHRĪ'S HISTORY

Mehmed Neşrî: Kitâb-ı Cihan-nümâ, Neşrî tarihi, ed. Faik Reşit Unat and Mehmed A. Köymen, i (pp. 1–420), Ankara, 1949; ii (pp. 421–844), Ankara, 1957 (= Türk Tarih Kurumu yayınlarından, III. seri, 2*a*, 2*b*). Abbreviation: *Ank.*

Ǧihānnümā: die altosmanische Chronik des Mevlānā Meḥemmed Neschrī, im Auftrage der Deutschen Akademie der Wissenschaften zu Berlin nach Vorarbeiten von Theodor Menzel herausgegeben von Franz Taeschner. Band I: Einleitung und Text des Cod. Menzel, Leipzig, 1951. Abbreviation: *Mz.*

Ǧihānnümā: . . . Band II: Text des Cod. Manisa 1373, Leipzig, 1955. Abbreviation: *Mn.*

II. OTHER HISTORICAL TEXTS

ʿĀLĪ, *Kunh al-akhbār*, 5 vols., Istanbul, 1277.

—— —— Istanbul, University Library MS. T 5959 (microfilm).

Almanac ('*taḳwīm*'). Dublin, Chester Beatty Library MS. 402 (photocopy).

—— Istanbul, Bağdad Köşkü Library MS. 309 (transcript).

—— Istanbul, Nur-i Osmaniye Library MS. 3080 (microfilm).

ʿĀSHIḲPASHAZĀDE (Aḥmed ʿĀshiḳī). *Die altosmanische Chronik des ʿĀšiḳpašazāde*, ed. F. Giese, Leipzig, 1929. Abbreviation: *ʿĀpz*, distinguished from the next, when necessary, as *ʿĀpz* (*G*).

—— *Tevārīkh-i Āl-i ʿOsmāndan ʿĀshiḳpashazāde taʾrīkhi*, ed. ʿĀlī, Istanbul, 1332.

ATSIZ, Ç. N. ed. 'Fatih Sultan Mehmed'e sunulmuş tarihî bir takvim', *İstanbul Enstitüsü Dergisi*, iii, 1957, 17–23.

—— *Osmanlı tarihine ait takvimler*, i, Istanbul, 1961.

—— *Osmanlı tarihleri*, i, Istanbul, 1949.

ʿAZĪZ B. ARDASHĪR. *Bazm u razm*, ed. Kilīsli Rifʿat, Istanbul, 1928.

BIHISHTĪ. History of the Ottoman Dynasty. British Museum MS. Add. 7869.

ENVERĪ. *Dustūr-nāme-i Enverī*, ed. Mükrimīn Khalīl [Yınanç], Istanbul, 1928.

GIESE, F. ed. *Die altosmanischen anonymen Chroniken*, in Text und Übersetzung herausgegeben von Dr. Friedrich Giese. Teil I: Text und Variantenverzeichnis, Breslau, 1922.

IBN BĪBĪ. *Ibn-i Bībī: El-Evāmirüʾl-ʿalāʾiyye fīʾl-umūriʾl-ʿAlāʾiyye*, i (tıpkıbasım), ed. Adnan Sadık Erzi, Ankara, 1956.

IDRĪS BIDLĪSĪ. *Hasht Bihisht*, British Museum MSS. Add. 7646, 7647.

KEMĀLPASHAZĀDE. *Ibn Kemal: Tevârih-i Âl-i Osman, VII. defter*, ed. Şerafettin Turan, Ankara, 1954.

LEUNCLAVIUS (Löwenklau), J. *Historiae musulmanae Turcorum, de monumentis ipsorum exscriptae, libri xviii*, Frankfurt, 1591. Abbreviation: *H.M.*

'NESHRĪ'. Paris, Bibliothèque Nationale MS. supp. turc 1183 (= MS. Pb), microfilm.

'RŪḤĪ'. Oxford, Bodleian Library MS. Marsh 313 (microfilm); referred to as the 'Oxford Anonymous History', abbreviation: O.A.

'RUSTEM PASHA'. *Die osmanische Chronik des Rustem Pascha*, abridged trans. by L. Forrer, Leipzig, 1923 (= Turk. Bibl. xxi).

SAʿDEDDĪN. *Tāj al-tawārīkh*, 2 vols., Istanbul, 1279–80.

SHUKRULLĀH. 'Der Abschnitt über die Osmanen in Šükrüllāh's persischer Universalgeschichte', ed. T. Seif, *Mitteilungen zur Osmanischen Geschichte*, ii, 1923–6, 63–128.

—— British Museum MS. Or. 11155 (anonymous Turkish translation of the Ottoman section of the *Bahjat al-tawārīkh*).

SOLAKZĀDE. *Ta'rīkh*, Istanbul, 1298.

TURAN, OSMAN ed. *İstanbul'un fethinden önce yazılmış tarihî takvimler*, Ankara, 1954.

URUJ. *Die frühosmanischen Jahrbücher des Urudsch*, ed. F. Babinger, Hanover, 1925.

III. STUDIES

AKIN, H. *Aydın Oğulları tarihi hakkında bir araştırma*, Istanbul, 1946.

ARIK, FAHRİYE. *Onbeşinci asır tarihçilerinden Neşrî'nin hayatı ve eserleri*, Istanbul, 1936.

BABINGER, F. 'Der Pfortendolmetsch Murād und seine Schriften', in *Literaturdenkmäler aus Ungarns Türkenzeit*, ed. E. Mittwoch and J. H. Mordtmann, Berlin and Leipzig, 1927.

GIESE, F. *Die verschiedenen Textrezensionen des ʿĀšiqpašazāde bei seinen Nachfolgern und Ausschreibern*, Abh. Pr. Ak. W., Jahrg. 1936, Phil.-hist. Kl., Nr. 4, Berlin, 1936.

HALIL [YINANÇ], MÜKRIMIN. *Düsturnamei Enverî: Medhal*, Istanbul, 1930.

INALCIK, H. *Fatih devri üzerinde tetkikler ve vesikalar*, i, Ankara, 1954.

——'The rise of Ottoman historiography', in *Historians of the Middle East*, ed. Bernard Lewis and P. M. Holt, London, 1962, 152–67.

LEVEND, AGÂH SIRRI. *Türk dilinde gelişme ve sadeleşme safhaları*, Ankara, 1949.

MÉNAGE, V. L. 'The beginnings of Ottoman historiography', in *Historians of the Middle East*, ed. Bernard Lewis and P. M. Holt, London, 1962, 168–79.

—— 'The *Menāqib* of Yakhshi Faqīh', *BSOAS*, xxvi, 1963, 50–54.

MORDTMANN, J. H. 'Rūḥī Edrenewī', *Mitteilungen zur Osmanischen Geschichte*, ii, 1923–6, 129–36.

ROSSI, E. 'Parafrasi turca del *de Senectute* presentata a Solimano il Magnifico dal Bailo Marino de' Cavalli (1559)', *Rendiconti della Reale*

Accademia Nazionale dei Lincei, Cl. di Scienze morali, storiche e filologiche, ser. 6, vol. xii, 1936, 680–756.

ŠÜKRÜ, M. 'Das Hešt Bihišt des Idrīs Bitlīsī', *Der Islam*, xix, 1931, 131–57.

TAESCHNER, F. 'Eine Ausgabe von Neschri's altosmanischer Chronik', *Der Islam*, xxix, 1950, 307–17.

—— 'Neşrî tarihi elyazıları üzerine araştırmalar', *Belleten*, xv, 1951, 497–505.

UNAT, F. R. 'Müverrih Mehmet Neşri'nin eseri ve hayatı hakkinda', *Belleten*, xxi, 1957, 297–300.

—— 'Neşrî tarihi üzerinde yapılan çalışmalara toplu bir bakış', *Belleten*, vii, 1943, 177–201.

WITTEK, P. *Das Fürstentum Mentesche: Studie zur Geschichte Westkleinasiens im 13.–15. Jh.* (Istanbuler Mitteilungen 2), Istanbul, 1934.

—— 'Die altosmanische Chronik des ʿĀšiḳpašazāde', *Orientalische Literaturzeitung*, xxxiv, 1931, cols. 698–707.

—— 'The taking of Aydos castle: a ghāzī legend and its transformation', to appear in a volume of studies in honour of Sir Hamilton Gibb.

—— 'Zum Quellenproblem der ältesten osmanischen Chroniken (mit Auszügen aus Nešrī)', *Mitteilungen zur Osmanischen Geschichte*, i, 1921–2, 77–150.

IV. WORKS OF REFERENCE AND CATALOGUES

BABINGER, F. *Die Geschichtsschreiber der Osmanen und ihre Werke*, Leiden, 1927.

BLOCHET, E. *Bibliothèque Nationale: catalogue des manuscrits turcs*, 2 vols., Paris, 1932–3.

Encyclopaedia of Islam (*new edition*), Leiden and London, 1954– .

FLÜGEL, G. *Die arabischen, persischen, und türkischen Handschriften der Kaiserlich-königlichen Hofbibliothek zu Wien*, 3 vols., Vienna, 1865–7.

FORRER, L. 'Handschriften osmanischer Historiker in Istanbul', *Der Islam*, xxvi, 1942, 173–220.

ḤĀJJĪ KHALFA, *Kashf al-ẓunūn. Lexicon bibliographicum et encyclopaedicum a Mustafa ben Abdallah . . . compositum*, ed. G. Flügel, 7 vols., Leipzig, 1835–58.

—— —— *Katib Çelebi: Keşf-el-zunun*, ed. Şerefettin Yaltkaya and Kilisli Rifat Bilge, 2 vols., Istanbul, 1941–3.

İslâm Ansiklopedisi, Istanbul, 1940– .

İstanbul kitaplıkları tarih-coğrafya yazmaları katalogları, i (türkçe tarih yazmaları), 10 fascicules, Istanbul, 1943–51.

KARATAY, F. E. *Topkapı Sarayı Müzesi Kütüphanesi: türkçe yazmalar kataloğu*, 2 vols., Istanbul, 1961.

LAṬĪFĪ. *Tez̤kere-i Laṭīfī*, Istanbul, 1314 (Kitābkhāne-i Iḳdām, no. 9).

MINORSKY, V. *The Chester Beatty Library: a catalogue of the Turkish manuscripts and miniatures*, Dublin, 1958.

PARMAKSIZOĞLU, I. *Manisa Genel Kütüphanesi: tarih-coğrafya yazmaları kataloğu*, Istanbul, 1952.

SMIRNOV, V. D. *Manuscrits turcs de l'Institut des Langues Orientales*, St. Petersburg, 1897.

ṬĀHIR, (BURSALI) MEḤMED. *ʿOs̲mānlı müʾellifleri*, 3 vols., Istanbul, 1333–42.

TASHKÖPRÜZĀDE, *al-Shaḳāʾiḳ al-nuʿmāniyya*. Turkish translation (*Ḥadāʾiḳ al-shaḳāʾiḳ*) by Mejdī, Istanbul, 1269.

—— —— German translation (*Eš-šaqāʾiq en-noʿmānijje von Tāšköprüzāde*) by O. Rescher, Istanbul, 1927.

INTRODUCTION

No other Ottoman historian has had so great an influence on later writers as Neshrī, who was working in the early years of the reign of Bāyezīd II (1481–1512). In the Ottoman Empire his work was used extensively by nearly all the historians of the Classical Age of literature which began during that reign; while in Europe, long before Hammer used it for his *Geschichte des osmanischen Reiches* (1828–35), Neshrī's account of events had been known from Leunclavius's *Historiae musulmanae Turcorum . . . libri xviii* (Frankfurt, 1591), which served as a main source of Richard Knolles's *Generall historie of the Turkes* (London, 1603, and numerous later editions).

Studies on the Turkish text of Neshrī's History were until recently centred on the Vienna manuscript (W), which had belonged to Hammer; excerpts from it were published by Behrnauer (1857), Nöldeke (1859, 1861), Smirnov (1903), and Wittek (1922), and Thury used it for his collection of translations of passages relating to Hungarian history (1893).[1] The systematic publication of the complete text began only in 1949 with the appearance of the first volume, containing slightly less than half the text, of an edition prepared for the Türk Tarih Kurumu by F. R. Unat and M. A. Köymen (*Ank*); the second volume (1957) ends with the account of the death of Meḥemmed II, so that only a small portion of text remains for the third volume, which will also contain notes and indexes. With eight manuscripts at their disposal, the Turkish editors followed tradition by basing their text on W—in fact an unfortunate decision;[2] and their edition, in Arabic script with Latin transcription on the facing pages, falls far short of the ideal. Some years earlier T. Menzel had prepared, mainly from an Istanbul manuscript, a text and German translation of Neshrī's History, but when he acquired the manuscript now known after him as the Codex Menzel (Mz), which was much older than any other extant, he felt obliged to undertake a revision. After his

[1] References to these and other studies are given by F. Taeschner, *Mz* (*Einl.*) (i.e. *Einleitung* to his facsimile of the Codex Menzel), 1–9.

[2] See F. Taeschner's review, 'Eine Ausgabe von Neschri's altosmanischer Chronik', *Der Islam*, xxix, 1949, 307–17.

death in 1939 his work was resumed at the invitation of the German Academy by Professor F. Taeschner, who in 1951 issued a facsimile (*Mz*) of Menzel's manuscript; in his introduction he showed that it represents an earlier recension of the text than that represented by the manuscripts used for *Ank.*[1] The second volume in the German series (1955) is a facsimile of the Manisa manuscript (*Mn*), which seems to be the next oldest, and the best witness to the text of the later recension; it possesses the further merit of being fully vocalized. The third volume is to be a reprint, with German translation, of those sections of the *Historiae musulmanae* which reflect Neshrī's work.

The great landmark in the critical study of the text is Professor P. Wittek's demonstration (1922), with extensive quotations, of the dependence of Neshrī's History on 'Āshiḳpashazāde's, and his investigation of its connexion with the *Historiae musulmanae.* In Turkey, Fahriye Arık published a study (1936) of what is known of Neshrī's life with an analysis of his account of the reigns of 'Os̱mān Ghāzī and Orkhān, and F. R. Unat a useful survey of the position reached by 1942. In the meantime more and more manuscripts of Neshrī's work have come to light, so that whereas in 1927 Professor F. Babinger could record only three,[2] no fewer than fourteen are now known.[3]

In recent years, indeed, a fresh assessment of the problems presented by Neshrī's History has become both necessary and possible. The new situation began with the appearance in 1929 of F. Giese's much superior edition of 'Āshiḳpashazāde's History, Neshrī's principal source. And now the two further sources used by Neshrī are—broadly at least—identified: Professor H. Inalcık showed in 1954 that Neshrī had used a chronological list ('*taḳwīm*') close to the two published in the same year by O. Turan,[4] and in 1958 Inalcık and I[5] independently stated the conclusion that

[1] Taeschner summarized his conclusions also in his 'Neşrî tarihi elyazıları üzerine araştırmalar,' *Belleten*, xv, 1951, 497–505.

[2] F. Babinger, *Die Geschichtsschreiber der Osmanen und ihre Werke*, Leiden, 1927, 38 f. (recording V, W, and Pb).

[3] Namely Mz, discussed here in Ch. IV; Mn, A[sariatika Müzesi], P[aris] a, W, V[eliyeddin], F[atih-Millet], E[sad Efendi], S[aray], N[öldeke], T[ürk Tarih Kurumu], and Y[ınanç], discussed in Ch. VI; P[aris] b and D[il Tarih-Coğrafya Fakültesi], discussed in Ch. VII.

[4] H. Inalcık, *Fatih devri*, 23.

[5] In papers contributed to the Conference on historical writing in the Near and Middle East (held at the School of Oriental and African Studies in July,

Neshrī had followed a text intimately related to an anonymous Turkish History of the Ottomans preserved in the Bodleian Library.

This text is the latest and fullest extant representative of a literary tradition which appears in the Ottoman sections of Aḥmedī's *Iskender-nāme* (*c.* 1405) and of Shukrullāh's *Bahjat al-tawārīkh* (1459), and is echoed in the first of Karamānī Meḥemmed Pasha's two *risāla*s (1480).[1] Beside this tradition there had developed a more popular one which can be traced back to an early recension—not extant in its original form—of the Anonymous Chronicles edited by F. Giese. This recension, composed shortly after the accession of Murād II (1421–51), was used by ʿĀshiḳpashazāde, who combined with it the *menāḳib* related in the lost work of Yakhshi Faḳīh (? *c.* 1405)[2] and appended to it his own account, mostly original, of the years down to his own day.

The two traditions developed separately, each receiving accretions at the hands of successive writers but neither influencing the other, until Neshrī, by using as his principal sources a text close to the Oxford Anonymous and ʿĀshiḳpashazāde's History in the recension edited by Giese, interwove them. Neshrī's History thus represents the nodal point of early Ottoman historical writings: in it for the first time the two traditions come together, and from it the conflated tradition, influencing already Idrīs and Kemālpashazāde, penetrates the works of most later writers.

It might seem that with Neshrī's sources thus identified the scholar may now ignore Neshrī's work and confine his attention to his sources, making his own assessment of their reliability unprejudiced by Neshrī's careful and ingenious attempt to harmonize them. This is largely true. But before dismissing Neshrī from consideration it is as well to survey the development of his work, as a guide to the study of other texts which may be presumed to have gone through similar stages at the hands of their authors and of copyists but for which less ample materials are available. Furthermore, Neshrī's text remains of value as being in effect

1958), since published in *Historians of the Middle East*, ed. Bernard Lewis and P. M. Holt, London, 1962, 152–67 (Inalcık), 168–79 (Ménage).

[1] See H. Inalcık, *Rise*, 159–62.

[2] See V. L. Ménage, 'The *menāqib* of Yakhshi Faqīh', *BSOAS*, xxvi, 1963, 50–54.

a contemporary commentary on the very difficult text of ʿĀshiḳ-pashazāde, while the obscurities which remain are frequently clarified by the admirable Latin version of the *Historiae musulmanae*. It is not then lost labour to compare the texts again in the light of the recent discoveries.

I

NESHRĪ'S LIFE

THE work known as 'Neshrī's History' owes its attribution to the appearance of the *makhlaṣ* 'Neshrī' in a short *ḳaṣīde* in praise of Bāyezīd II (1481–1512), which in some manuscripts closes the work. A poet writing under this *makhlaṣ* is recorded in the *tezkeres*,[1] but even Laṭīfī, the earliest of the biographers to mention him (1546), reports of his life only that he came from Karaman and died in the reign of Selīm I (1512–20).[2] Laṭīfī's low opinion of his poetical talent was evidently shared by his contemporaries, for nothing is known to survive of his poems beyond the *ḳaṣīde*, the lines quoted by the biographers, and a few scattered lines of verse—if these are original—introduced into the History.

That Neshrī the historian and Neshrī the poet are, as 'Ālī assumed, the same man there is no reason to doubt. In his work he tells us only that he had been interested 'all his life' in history (*Mz* 2, 18/*Ank* 6, 1)—a phrase which suggests that in the early years of Bāyezīd's reign, when he was writing, he had already reached a mature age—and that he was present in the Ottoman camp near Gebze on the night when Meḥemmed II died (4 Rebīʿ I 886/3 May 1481): he was sleeping near the tent of the 'Ṣāḥib-i 'ayār' (the master-assayer,[3] presumably of the Istanbul mint), who woke him with the news that the dignitaries had all struck camp and gone; Neshrī, making his way to Üsküdar, managed to cross to Istanbul, where he witnessed the riots of the Janissaries (*Mz* 219, 8 ff.). He does not reveal in what capacity he was taking part in the campaign, nor does he hint elsewhere that he was a witness of any of the events which he describes.

[1] The sparse and contradictory evidence for Neshrī's life, from sources mostly still unpublished, has most recently been collected together by Fahriye Arık and by F. R. Unat (*Bakış*), upon whose studies depend F. Taeschner's survey, in *Mz* (*Einl.*), 9–14, and M. C. Şehâbeddin Tekindağ's article, s.v. Neşrî, in *IA*.

[2] *Tezkere-i Laṭīfī*, Istanbul, 1314, 333–4. Laṭīfī is followed by 'Ahdī (whose *tezkere* was completed in 971/1563) and Riyāżī (1018/1609).

[3] See *EI*² s.v. Dār al-ḍarb (H. Inalcık), col. 118*b*.

The biographers, it is true, claim to know something more about him, but the details which they give are at variance. Whereas Laṭīfī says that he came from Karaman, according to ʿĀshik̲ Čelebi he was a man of Bursa; ʿĀlī makes him a native of 'a town in Anatolia', and Evliyā of Germiyan. The earliest tradition, that he came from Karaman, gains some support from the fact that Neshrī shows an interest in the affairs of that principality: he introduces a short history of it into the second section of the surviving volume of his work (*Mz* 15, 17–17, 7/*Ank* 42, 16–48, 10), and at a few points in his section on the Ottomans he expands his account of events in Karaman with details not found in his known sources.[1] The tradition that he lived at Bursa, though relatively late—appearing first in ʿĀshik̲ Čelebi's *tezkere*, of 1568, it is repeated by ʿĀlī and Evliyā—is similarly supported by some details in the text of his History: of the three informants whom he names, Mevlānā Ayās was resident there and Meḥemmed b. Ḳuṭbeddīn at the near-by Iznik;[2] the earlier recension of his work contains some details, lacking in Neshrī's sources, which would be familiar to one living in Bursa;[3] and the manuscripts of the later recension too contain further hints that the reviser—who must, as will appear, be Neshrī himself—was acquainted with the history and topography of the town.[4] It may also be inferred, from the style and content of Neshrī's introduction to his work, that he was a member of the ʿulemā, with a knowledge of Arabic and Persian;[5] but Ḥājjī K̲h̲alfa's assertion that he was a *müderris* (with the personal name Meḥemmed)[6] is, we shall see, open to question.

---

[1] See below, p. 18.

[2] Mevlānā Ayās, for whom see Tashköprüzāde (Rescher), 109 = (Mejdī), 189 f., is named (and there called '*merḥūm*') at *Mz* 20, 16/*Ank* 60, 19 as the authority for a story of Ertog̲h̲rul's rescuing Sultan ʿAlāeddīn's army in a skirmish with Mongols. Meḥ. b. Ḳuṭbeddīn, for whom see Tashköprüzāde (Rescher), 63 f. = (Mejdī), 124 f., ʿ*OM*, i. 159 f., is cited (*Mz* 97, 10/*Ank* 358, 11) for the story, which he had heard from his father, of an unsuccessful attempt to ransom Bāyezīd I from Timur.

[3] See below, p. 18.

[4] See below, pp. 41–42.

[5] For the Ottoman portion of his History, the bulk of what survives, he used only Turkish sources (see Ch. III), but the earlier books of his *Jihān-numā*, which are lost, must have been largely based on Arabic and Persian works. His reference (*Ank* 6, 5–6) to the inadequacy of existing historical works 'especially in Turkish' also points to an acquaintance with the classical languages of Islam.

[6] *Kashf al-ẓunūn*, ed. Flügel, no. 2155 = ed. Yaltkaya and Bilge, i. 284.

Various attempts have been made to supplement this meagre biography, but none of them stands up to critical examination. Firstly, J. H. Mordtmann noticed a certain 'Meḥemmed b. Neshrī' listed in the printed text of 'Ālī's *Kunh al-akhbār* (v. 225) among the 'ulemā who flourished under Murād II: he might, he suggested,[1] be a relative, perhaps the grandfather, of the historian. As Fahriye Arık has pointed out, however, the biography there given to this 'Meḥemmed b. Neshrī'—he came to Bursa when young and rose to be *müderris* of the '*Sulṭān medresesi*' there—is in fact a summary of that given in the *Shaḳā'iḳ al-nu'māniyya*, 'Ālī's main source for his biographies of 'ulemā, to Meḥemmed b. Beshīr,[2] so that the 'b. Neshrī' of the printed text of 'Ālī is merely a corruption for 'b. Beshīr'.

But the confusion goes further than this. 'Ālī, noting that he had also written a History of the Ottoman House, records our Neshrī in his list of the poets of the reign of Selīm I; but in at least one manuscript of the *Kunh al-akhbār*[3] the *makhlaṣ* 'Neshrī', certainly the original reading,[4] has been replaced—presumably under the influence of the earlier misreading—by 'Meḥemmed b. Neshrī'. Misled by a manuscript containing this further corruption, Bursalı Meḥmed Ṭāhir records of the historian, whom he calls 'Neshrī Meḥemmed Efendi', that he came to Bursa and lived there as *müderris* of the '*Sulṭāniyye medresesi*',[5] details which in fact belong to Meḥemmed b. Beshīr and have no application to the historian. Again, it is probable that Ḥājjī Khalfa's report that Neshrī's personal name was Meḥemmed and that he was a *müderris*, for which no other possible source is known, depends

[1] *Der Islam*, xiii, 1923, 167, in the course of his review of P. Wittek's *Quellenproblem*.

[2] Tashköprüzāde (Rescher), 46 = (Mejdī), 100 (followed also by Sa'deddīn, ii. 439); the full entry makes clear that the '*Sulṭān medresesi*' of 'Ālī is the *medrese* of Bāyezīd I.

[3] Quoted by F. R. Unat, *Bakış*, 178, n. 5.

[4] 'Ālī's practice is to list each poet according to his *makhlaṣ* only, without a personal name or patronymic. The Vienna MS. (quoted by P. Wittek, *Quellenproblem*, 82, n. 2) has as heading simply 'Neshrī', as has, I find, the Istanbul University MS. T 5959 (fol. 210*v*.).

[5] '*OM*, iii. 150, where also is reported a tradition that Neshrī's grave had been known at Bursa, but was destroyed when a road was widened; this seems very dubious, for a *makhlaṣ* is unlikely to have figured on a tombstone. Fahriye Arık is mistaken in saying (p. 4) that according to Flügel's catalogue of the Vienna MSS. ii. 209, Neshrī mentions in his History that he was a *müderris* at the '*Sulṭān medresesi*'. Flügel makes no such statement; she must have had '*OM* in mind.

on a corrupt manuscript of the *Kunh al-akhbār* in which the biography of Meḥemmed b. Beshīr had been given to 'Meḥemmed b. Neshrī'.

In an entry, dated 884/1479, in the registers of the Ḳāḍī of Bursa is found the name 'Neshrī Ḥuseyn b. Eyne Beg',[1] and F. Taeschner (accepting that Neshrī's own name was Meḥemmed) has suggested that he may be a relative of the historian. But 'Neshrī' cannot be a family-name, of the order of 'Āshiḳī and Fenārī, nor an abbreviated *laḳab* like Sa'dī and Shemsī, for the name 'Neshr' or 'Neshreddīn' is non-existent: it can only be a *makhlaṣ*, in which case this Ḥuseyn must be either completely unconnected with the historian or identical with him. In view of the date of the entry and the rarity of the *makhlaṣ*—no other user of it is known—it is not improbable that this record does refer to our Neshrī.

Taeschner has also suggested[2] that Neshrī must have been already adult as early as the reign of Murād II, on the ground that he names as an informant a certain Koja Nā'ib, who was, as an old man, *nā'ib* of Bursa early in Murād's reign. But this reference (*Mz* 96, 18 ff./*Ank* 354, 9 ff.) Neshrī has taken over almost verbatim from his principal source, 'Āshiḳpashazāde's History ('*Āpz* 71, 13 ff.), so that it is no evidence that Neshrī had known him personally. Of the three persons who were indeed Neshrī's direct informants, Meḥemmed b. Ḳuṭbeddīn died in 885/1480–1, right at the end of Meḥemmed II's reign, Mevlānā Ayās seems to have lived on into the reign of Bāyezīd II, and Turakhān Beg-oghlu 'Omer Beg was still alive in 894/1489.[3]

F. R. Unat has now claimed[4] that a series of autobiographical references, found in a continuation appended to an abridged version of Neshrī's work, were made by Neshrī himself; but examination of them (see Ch. VII) shows that this is hardly possible.

We are left therefore with little more than what emerges from the History: its author's *makhlaṣ* was Neshrī; he was a member of

[1] Communication of H. Inalcık to F. Taeschner, see *Mn* (*Einl.*), 2, n. 1.

[2] *Mz* (*Einl.*), 10 f.

[3] Meḥ. b. Ḳuṭbeddīn's death in 885 is recorded by Neshrī, *Mz* 218, 1/*Ank* 838, 12. Mevlānā Ayās is said to have accompanied Seljuk Khātūn on her embassy from Jem to Bāyezīd in 886 (*Mn* 312, 2, whereas *Mz* 221, 1, following '*Āpz* 184, 8, names Shukrullāh-oghlu Aḥmed Čelebi; M. Ayās is named also by Idrīs [see F. Giese, *Textrez.*, 11] and hence by Sa'deddīn, ii. 10). 'Omer Beg is named among the commanders in a campaign of 894 ('*Āpz* 232, 8 ff.).

[4] In *Belleten*, xxi, 1957, 297–300: see below, p. 54.

the 'ulemā; he was with the Ottoman army when Meḥemmed II died; and he was writing in the early years of Bāyezīd II's reign. To this we may add that he was a minor poet; that he lived at Bursa; and, with less certainty, Laṭīfī's statements that he hailed from Karaman and died during the reign of Selīm I. His personal name may, on the evidence of the Bursa register, have been Ḥuseyn b. Eyne Beg. The very meagreness of the references to him show that he lived a quiet and obscure life and enjoyed little contemporary fame.

II

THE *JIHĀN-NUMĀ*

How Neshrī came to compose his History he relates in its introduction (*Ank* 6). He had found that, whereas for other sciences many adequate compendia existed, the current historical works, especially those in Turkish, were dispersed and not assembled together (or perhaps 'lacking in agreement': *ghayr-i mujtemi'*) and the events were not arranged correctly. So he drafted a history of the whole world, from the Creation down to his own day, to which he gave the name *Jihān-numā*, 'Cosmorama'. The fair copy of this *Jihān-numā* was completed in the reign of Bāyezīd II (so at least say some of the manuscripts: to the variant 'Meḥemmed II' found in one we shall return). Later the sixth and last section (*ḳism*) of the *Jihān-numā*, devoted to the history of the descendants of Oghuz Khān, he separated off (*ifrāz etdüm*) from the parent-work for presentation to Bāyezīd. It is this sixth section which is represented by the surviving manuscripts of 'Neshrī's History'.

No manuscript of any of the first five sections of the *Jihān-numā* is known to survive,[1] nor, apparently, were they known to Ḥājjī Khalfa,[2] but some idea of their scope can be gathered from

[1] Professor Wittek has drawn my attention, however, to V. D. Smirnov's description of a manuscript which contains an anonymous and undated Turkish history of the Abbasids, ending with an uncompleted chapter on the conquest of Baghdad by the Mongols (*Manuscrits turcs de l'Institut des Langues Orientales*, St. Petersburg, 1897, 10–13 and plates I, II*a*, II*b*). Its main heading is وطبقه ثالثه خلفاء عباسيه بيان ادر, precisely the style that Neshrī uses at *Mz* 8, 17/*Ank* 22 and *Mz* 18, 19/*Ank* 54; some chapters are introduced by words used also by Neshrī, e.g. مورخ ايدر (cf. *Ank* 12, 14; 18, 17). It was composed after the capture of Constantinople and is written on paper whose watermarks date it to the end of the fifteenth century. From the numerous corrections in the same hand as the text it appears to be the author's draft. This might indeed be Neshrī's '*ṭabaḳa* on the Abbasids'.

[2] In a reference to Neshrī's *Jihān-numā* which appears in the margin of the autograph of the *Kashf al-ẓunūn* (MS. Revan 2059, fol. 254*r*, cited by F. R. Unat, *Bakış*, 180; it is incorporated in the text of Flügel's MS. B, see his edition, no. 4356) Ḥājjī Khalfa says that it was 'composed in the reign of Meḥemmed II, and the sixth section, the section devoted to the Ottomans and the Seljuks of Rūm, in the reign of Bāyezīd II'. Unat takes this as an indication that the complete

three 'cross-references' left unexpunged in the 'History of the Oghuzian Turks': these references, to 'the second *ṭabaḳa* ('stratum, layer') of the first *ḳism* of this book *Jihān-numā*, on the descendants of Noah' (*Mz* 19, 14/*Ank* 56, 8), to its '*ṭabaḳa* on the Abbasids' (*Mz* 13, 12/*Ank* 36, 10) and to its 'fifth *ḳism*' on the rise of the Seljuk dynasty (*Mz* 10, 1/*Ank* 26, 4), suffice to show that the *Jihān-numā* had indeed been a Universal History on the model of classical Arabic and Persian works, perhaps the first to be written in Turkish prose.

The sixth section consists of the introduction and three *ṭabaḳa*. The introduction, written in a much more elevated style than the body of the work, consists of a short *tevḥīd* and *na'͑t*, followed by a discourse on the value of learning, particularly its highest branches, theology, jurisprudence, and history, and the necessity that princes should study them. It seems a reasonable assumption that this is the original introduction to the *Jihān-numā*, copied out, with the addition of the sentence mentioning the 'separation' of the sixth section (*Ank* 6, 12–15), to stand at the head of the now independent History of the Turks.

The first *ṭabaḳa* is a very summary account of the ancestors and descendants of Oghuz Khān and of the Karakhānid dynasty, the second an equally brief history of the Great Seljuks leading into a somewhat more detailed account of the Seljuks of Rūm down to the break-up of their state after the Mongol invasions; into the latter is interpolated a history of the House of Karaman from its origins to the beginning of the eighth/fourteenth century. These two *ṭabaḳa* together form less than a tenth of the surviving section. The third *ṭabaḳa* recounts the history of the Ottomans from the legendary beginnings of the dynasty down to the first years of the reign of Bāyezīd II, the latest date being 25 Sha'bān 890/6 Sept. 1485. After 'summary chapters' on the pious works of the viziers and on the holy men who flourished in each reign, the work ends with an account of the pious foundations of Bāyezīd II and the short *ḳaṣīde* in his praise in which the author's *makhlaṣ* appears.

The composition of a work as extensive as the *Jihān-numā* must have been begun many years before the latest events recorded in it; Neshrī, indeed, says as much in commenting that 'all his life'

Jihān-numā was known to Ḥājjī Khalfa; but the entry seems to be merely an inference which Ḥājjī Khalfa has drawn from Neshrī's introduction.

he had been eager to compose a comprehensive history. A variant reading in one early manuscript however implies that the whole work—necessarily in a somewhat less extended form than what survives—had been completed already in the reign of Meḥemmed II. For whereas some manuscripts[1] speak of the fair copy being made 'in the days of Sulṭān Bāyezīd Khān Ghāzī b. Sulṭān Meḥemmed Khān Ghāzī', the Codex Manisa reads here 'Sulṭān Meḥemmed b. Murād Khān Ghāzī' (*Mn* 2, 19). This reading the Turkish editors have adopted in their text (*Ank* 6, 10).

In his review of *Ank*[2] F. Taeschner posed the question whether Mn in fact represented an earlier recension prepared for Meḥemmed II or whether Mn's reading here arose merely from a copyist's omission of the words 'Sulṭān Bāyezīd Khān Ghāzī ibn'; and in his introduction to the facsimile of Mn (p. 4), though it was now clear that Mn's text did not differ substantially from that of other manuscripts, he again left the question open, pointing out that as our text embraces only the first years of the reign of Bāyezīd II the bulk of it could well have been completed under Meḥemmed II.

However, our text of Neshrī depends almost entirely upon two sources—the History of 'Āshiḳpashazāde and the Oxford Anonymous History—which (though earlier recensions of them may well have existed) were used by Neshrī in recensions completed only in or after 890/1485, the fifth year of Bāyezīd II's reign. Moreover, the 'History of the Oghuzian Turks' presented to Bāyezīd II was no entirely new work, but little more than section six of the *Jihān-numā*, 'separated off', as Neshrī expressly says and as is shown by the survival in the text of the cross-references to earlier books of 'this *Jihān-numā*'. Thus the Ottoman *ṭabaḳa*, by far the longest of the three parts forming the sixth section, could not have been written under Meḥemmed II, for the sources which Neshrī used for it had not then been composed.

Two explanations of Mn's variant are possible. It may be no more than an error by the copyist, whose eye has jumped from one '*Sulṭān*' to the next; this is improbable, for although the text of Mn contains many examples of the omission of one element of a

[1] Namely Pa and V. Mz, W, F, and A are defective here. Pb, on which see Ch. VII, reads 'Selīm Khān b. Bāyezīd'.

[2] F. Taeschner, 'Eine Ausgabe von Neschrī's altosmanischen Chronik', *Der Islam*, xxix, 1949–50, 307–17.

personal name[1] it seems unlikely that a copyist, however careless, should drop the name of the sultan to whom the work is dedicated. Alternatively, as Professor Wittek has suggested to me, this fully-vocalized manuscript might have been prepared as a text-book for one of the Ottoman princes during his stay at Manisa, the usual seat of the 'heir-apparent' during the sixteenth century, in which case Mn's reading could be a conscious alteration made in order to show the work as having been written in the reign of the prince's illustrious ancestor Meḥemmed II rather than under the pacific Bāyezīd. In either case it is certainly a deviation from the original 'Bāyezīd b. Meḥemmed'.

The terminus for the completion of the *Jihān-numā* can in fact be brought down a little further than the latest date mentioned in its text. Neshrī's 'summary-chapters' on the viziers and the 'ulemā closely reproduce 'Āshiḳpashazāde's, but he makes a few modifications to bring them up to date. Among these are references to Ibrāhīm Čandarlı being appointed vizier (*Mz* 229, 15; cf. *'Āpz* 197, 4, where he is still ḳāḍī'asker) and to Khādim 'Alī Beg being appointed vizier in succession to Fenārī-oghlu Aḥmed Pasha (*Mz* 231, 21, with the *du'ā* اعلّه الله محله, cf. *'Āpz* 199, 13).[2] Ibrāhīm is reported to have become vizier in Ṣafar 891, and Khādim 'Alī in 892.[3] The completion of the *Jihān-numā* falls, therefore, between 892 (beginning 28 Dec. 1486) and Rebī' II 898/Feb. 1493, the date appearing in the colophon of Mz, the earliest dated manuscript.

[1] The first few pages show, for example: *Mn* 7,12/*Mz* 7,20 محمود ⟨بن⟩ سبكتكين; *Mn* 10, 4/*Mz* 9, 19 جعفر for داود جغرى; *Mn* 10, 17/*Mz* 10, 9 ملك ⟨شاه⟩; *Mn* 12, 12/*Mz* 11, 15 غياث شاه ⟨سليمان⟩ ركن الدين ملك; *Mn* 16, 14/*Mz* 14, 19 ملك الطاهر قرارى for ملك الطاهر بيبرس; *Mn* 16, 18/*Mz* 15, 1 كيخسرو ⟨الدين⟩; *Mn* 22, 3/*Mz* 18, 16 مسعود بن ⟨كيكاوس و⟩ كيقباد بندقدارى; *Mn* 28, 5 & 8/*Mz* 23, 11 & 13 علا الدين ⟨كيقباد⟩ بن. This is evidence of hasty work by a careless copyist.

[2] The modifications may, it is true, have already stood in the manuscript of 'Āpz which Neshrī used, but even so their significance for dating the Neshrī text is not invalidated. They are found also in *Mn* 321, 10 and 324, 3 and in MS. W (see F. Giese, *Textrez.*, 49–50), which, however, have some further additions —these perhaps introduced by copyists—not found in Mz.

[3] Sa'deddīn, ii. 217, 218.

III

NESHRĪ'S SOURCES FOR HIS *ṬABAḲA* ON THE OTTOMANS

(1) *ʿĀshiḳpashazāde's History*

MODERN studies on the text of Neshrī are based on P. Wittek's fundamental article 'Zum Quellenproblem der ältesten osmanischen Chroniken', of 1922. Comparing the texts of Neshrī, as represented by the Vienna manuscript (W), ʿĀshiḳpashazāde, as represented by the Constantinople edition (C), and the Codex Hanivaldanus (on which see Ch. V, below), as represented in Leunclavius's *Historiae Musulmanae*, he summed up his conclusions in this schema (*Quellenproblem*, 148):

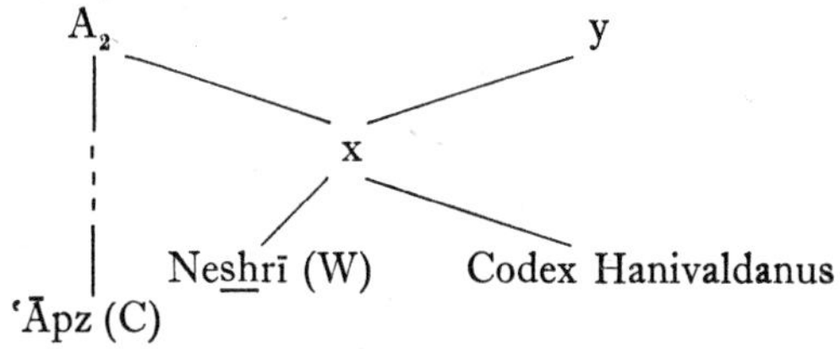

i.e., on the evidence of the texts available to him, ʿĀpz (C), in which the historical account reaches to the year 908/1502, derived from an archetype A_2, an earlier recension of ʿĀpz's History reaching to 890/1485, from which independently derived x (a compilation from A_2 and one or more other sources); while from x derived independently the relevant portions of the Codex Hanivaldanus and the Ottoman *ṭabaḳa* of Neshrī's History. The appearance of new manuscripts and editions corroborates this filiation of the texts.

The first confirmation came with the publication of F. Giese's edition of ʿĀpz, based on manuscripts in which the historical account ends, at the point Wittek had postulated, with the events of 890/1485. This recension is, as Giese claimed,[1] the text which

[1] F. Giese, *ʿĀpz* (*Einl.*), 22, and *Textrez.*, 46–50.

Neshrī used; so that 'A$_2$' in the schema may be replaced by ''Āpz, ed. Giese'.

(11) *The Oxford Anonymous History*

The Ottoman History of Rūḥī of Edirne, previously known only from citations in the works of 'Ālī and Münejjimbashı, was identified by J. H. Mordtmann,[1] who showed that a manuscript formerly owned by his father and later in the Berlin Staatsbibliothek, a prose History of the Ottomans reaching to 917/1511, contained all the passages which the later writers quoted as being taken from the work of Rūḥī. Mordtmann mentioned other manuscripts—one in Algiers and one in Oxford (Bodleian Library, MS. Marsh 313)—which seemed, from catalogue descriptions, to contain the same work. Comparison of these three manuscripts (of which, by the courtesy of the respective librarians, I have microfilms)[2] shows that only the Berlin and Algiers manuscripts represent the work of Rūḥī: the Oxford manuscript contains an earlier text, which served as the basis for the expanded and extended text referred to by 'Ālī and Münejjimbashı as 'Rūḥī's History'.

The anonymous author of the Oxford text says of himself only that his family 'has from of old been fostered by the bounty of the Ottoman House' and that he is in the service of Bāyezīd II, at whose prompting he wrote the work.[3] These words, taken in conjunction with the elaborate prose-style of his preface, suggest that he came of a family of chancery officials.

His work consists of a preface, two chapters called *mebādi'*, 'preliminaries', and eight longer sections called *maṭālib*, 'questions, problems', each of the latter being devoted to the reign of one sultan; the last (reign of Bāyezīd II) ends with Bāyezīd's return to Edirne from the campaign against Kili and Akkerman, for which it gives, as its latest date, 'end of Sha'bān 889' (= Sept. 1484).[4]

The preface, written in elaborate Turkish prose diversified with Koranic texts and a few lines of Arabic and Persian verse, is composed according to the traditional arrangement, with the praises

[1] J. H. Mordtmann, 'Rūḥī Edrenewī', *Mitt. z. Osm. Gesch.*, ii, 1923–6, 129–36.

[2] I hope to publish an edition of these texts in the near future.

[3] The relevant sections of the preface are quoted in Appendix II, pp. 70–71, below.

[4] See Appendix II, p. 75.

of God, the Prophet, and the reigning Sultan. In its last lines, after giving the few hints about himself noted above, the author says that Bāyezīd had, in the course of conversation, suggested that he should put together the History of the Ottoman House, 'which had never been done in a fitting fashion in Turkish'. He has therefore collected together those stories which are to be regarded as authentic (neither here nor elsewhere does he name a source) and related them concisely and without elaboration, desiring to give a clear and comprehensible account which the Sultan will approve. This indeed he has done: contenting himself with displaying in the few pages of the preface his abilities as a stylist, he writes the body of the work in simple and unpretentious Turkish.

The first of the two 'preliminary chapters' relates the virtues of the Ottoman House and the reasons for their pre-eminence over other Muslim dynasties: as descendants of Kayı, the eldest son of Oghuz, the Ottoman Sultans hold dominion not by usurpation but by right of seniority; their territory consists mostly of lands conquered from the infidel, their revenue arises mostly from the *jizye*. The second 'preliminary chapter', on the genealogy of the Ottomans, consists mostly of the story of how Jacob cheated Esau of his birthright, the relevance of which appears in a long genealogy (but without Kayı!) showing 'Osmān's father Ertoghrul to be descended from Shem through 'Gök Alp b. Oghuz b. Kara (?) Khān b. Koy Khān, which in the Coptic tongue means Esau'. The chapter then describes Ertoghrul's exploits in the service of the Seljuk Sultan 'Alāeddīn and the election of 'Osmān as Khan by the Turkish begs of the marches; a survey of the principalities then existing in Anatolia is interrupted by a lacuna in the manuscript: several pages have been lost, taking with them the whole of the first *maṭlab* ('Osmān Ghāzī) and the beginning of the second (Orkhān).

The remainder of the text (it resumes with Orkhān's capture of Iznik in 731) gives a detailed account of Ottoman history down to the author's day. Its most striking feature is the disproportionate length—over a third of the surviving text—accorded to the recital of Meḥemmed I's battles with various Turcoman chieftains and with his brothers (the fifth *maṭlab*).

The text with which this Oxford Anonymous History (hereafter O.A.) shows the closest and most extensive affinity is Shukrullāh's section on the Ottomans in his *Bahjat al-tawārīkh*, several passages in the Turkish, from the story of Ertoghrul's arrival in Rūm right down to the account of the death of Meḥemmed I, reading almost as translations of Shukrullāh's Persian. At the same time O.A.'s account is much longer and more detailed than Shukrullāh's, so that the connexion between them cannot be a direct dependence; it is probable that O.A. takes its account of events up to the end of the reign of Meḥemmed I from the source, apparently reaching only to that point,[1] which Shukrullāh used: the latter abridged it, whereas O.A. reproduces it more fully.

Into the first pages of this early part the author of O.A. has interpolated some passages—e.g. the 'election of 'Osmān' and the account of the principalities—evidently taken from Yazıjı-oghlu 'Alī's *Oghuz-nāme*.[2] His next source seems to have ended with the account of the events of 850/1446, for this is followed immediately by a chapter on the pious foundations of Murād II, whose position is explicable only as a survival from an earlier text of which it had formed the closing chapter. This explanation is supported by the fact that the 'pious foundations' are followed by a group of chapters which, as H. Inalcık has pointed out,[3] agree almost verbatim with 'Āpz's §§119–22: his convincing explanation is that the two writers have here independently incorporated into their Histories a short work of the *ghazā-nāme* type, recording the eventful years before and after the second battle of Kosova (852/1448).

A text very close to, but not identical with, that of O.A. served as Neshrī's second principal source. Wittek's comparison of Neshrī (W) and 'Āpz (C) revealed, besides numerous short passages for which Neshrī had had recourse to another source, two long sections of his text which are completely unconnected with 'Āpz. The first describes Murād I's campaigns against Karaman and in the Balkans, the second the vicissitudes of Meḥemmed I after the battle of Ankara.[4] As Wittek pointed out[5] and Taeschner

[1] Shukrullāh gives virtually no factual information on the reign of Murād II.

[2] See H. Inalcık, *Rise*, 160. Yazıjı-oghlu's account of the election of 'Osmān has been published by A. S. Levend, in transcription after MSS. Revan 1390 and 1391, in *Türk dilinde gelişme ve sadeleşme safhaları*, Ankara, 1949, 34 f., and his account of the principalities in part by M. Halil [Yınanç], *Düsturnamei Enveri: Medhal*, Istanbul, 1930, 13, and in full by P. Wittek, *Das Fürstentum Mentesche*, Istanbul, 1934, 33.

[3] *Rise*, 161 f.

[4] See *Quellenproblem*, 107–9 and 113–14. In the texts since published these sections occupy *Mz* 58–83/*Ank* 214–304 and *Mz* 98–141/*Ank* 366–516 respectively.

[5] *Quellenproblem*, 144.

has since remarked,[1] these two long 'interpolations' are written in a more elevated and discursive style than the sections derived from 'Āpz. One characteristic of the second is that in it the chapter-headings (for which elsewhere Neshrī usually uses Arabic or Persian) are invariably in Turkish, each ending with the archaic construction *-duğıdur/-düğidür*.

This construction appears consistently in the chapter-headings of O.A. Comparison of its text with Neshrī's shows that it includes, practically verbatim, the whole of the 'second interpolation'; the 'first interpolation', however, appears only in an abridged form, so that the text appearing in the Oxford manuscript cannot have served as Neshrī's immediate source. Nevertheless his source was very close to O.A., for in the latter, told in much the same words, are to be found nearly all the major episodes in Neshrī which are not derived from 'Āpz, from the chapter on Ertoghrul's capture of Karaja-ḥiṣār at the beginning of the *ṭabaḳa* down to that on Bāyezīd II's rebuilding of the Danube fortresses right at the end. There are also numerous resemblances of detail to show that Neshrī was using the tradition preserved in O.A. to amplify or modify the account supplied by 'Āpz.[2]

(III) *A chronological list*

In the first pages of some almanacs belonging to the reigns of Meḥemmed I, Murād II, and Meḥemmed II, the surviving examples of a series prepared, probably annually, to provide the Palace with astrological guidance for the following year, are found tabulated lists of historical events. The earliest known example is in Persian, the language of their non-Ottoman—perhaps Seljuk—model; the rest are in Turkish. They consist of numerous short entries, each recording concisely an accession, a death, a disaster or a battle, dated not by Hijra years but by the number of years elapsed since it occurred. Beginning with the Creation, they proceed through the Prophets and the pre-Islamic and early Islamic dynasties to the Seljuks, and so, with a list for Karaman sometimes included, to the Ottomans. The Ottoman sections begin with the

[1] *Mz* (*Einl.*), 13 f.

[2] See the concordance, Appendix I, pp. 58–69, and the specimens of the text of O.A. in Appendix II, pp. 70–75.

emergence (*khurūj*) of 'Osmān Ghāzī and gradually become more detailed, recording events in other parts of the Muslim world, as they approach the time of the compiler. He, we may assume, was the Court astrologer.[1]

Seven of these lists are so far known. The earliest, the only one in Persian, appears in an almanac made for Meḥemmed I for the year 824 (beginning 6 Jan. 1421); it has recently been published by Ç. N. Atsız, together with two further early specimens: a list for 835 (beg. 9 Sept. 1431) found in a *mejmū'a*, and one for 843 (beg. 14 June 1439) found in an almanac prepared for Murād II.[2] The *mejmū'a*'s list for 835 proves to be the same as that found in a sumptuous manuscript in the Chester Beatty collection.[3] Two more of Murād II's almanacs are known, one (in Paris) for 849 (beg. 9 Apr. 1445), the other (in Oxford) for 850 (beg. 29 Mar. 1446); their lists, the first to be made known, were published by O. Turan in 1954.[4] Of Meḥemmed II's almanacs two survive in Istanbul. MS. Bağdad Köşkü 309 is for 856 (beg. 23 Jan. 1452): the Ottoman section of its list, reproduced in part by H. Inalcık,[5] has been published in transcription by Atsız.[6] MS. Nur-i Osmaniye 3080 is for 858 (beg. 1 Jan. 1454.)[7]

The content of the Ottoman (as of the other) sections varies relatively slightly in the extant texts; they evidently derive ultimately from a single original, a list of events dated by Hijra years which was computed by the compiler of the first Ottoman almanac into the 'retrospective' system, to be appended to the retrospective lists already to hand in the model. Thereafter, in principle, the compiler of each new almanac needed only to take the copy for an earlier year and reproduce its list, adding the necessary figure to the number of 'years elapsed' since each event and appending

[1] For the antecedents and characteristics of these almanacs see O. Turan's introduction to his edition of the Paris and Oxford texts and H. Inalcık, *Rise*, 157 f.

[2] [Ç. N.] Atsız, *Osmanlı tarihine ait takvimler*, i, Istanbul, 1961.

[3] MS. Chester Beatty 402, described by V. Minorsky, *The Chester Beatty Library: a catalogue of the Turkish manuscripts and miniatures*, Dublin, 1958, 3 ff. By the kindness of the Honorary Librarian and of Dr. T. O. Gandjei I have photographs of the relevant pages of this manuscript.

[4] O. Turan, *Istanbul fethinden önce yazılmış tarihî takvimler*, Ankara, 1954.

[5] H. Inalcık, *Fatih devri*, pl. I.

[6] [Ç. N.] Atsız, 'Fatih Sultan Mehmed'e sunulmuş tarihî bir takvim', *İstanbul Enstitüsü Dergisi*, iii, 1957, 17–23.

[7] Of this manuscript, mentioned by M. Şehabeddin Tekindağ in *IA*, fasc. 59, col. 329*b*, I have a microfilm.

new paragraphs to bring it up to date. In theory, therefore, it should be possible, by tabulating the events and making the necessary subtractions from the years to which the almanacs belong, to construct a consistent table of Hijra dates; in practice, however, so many corruptions have arisen, from compilers' running two items together here and there, misplacing items, or occasionally forgetting to adjust the figures as necessary, that this is, at least with the available data, impossible.

One of these chronological lists was used by Neshrī. In his analysis of Neshrī's text Wittek drew attention to a series of short entries, usually beginning with the words 'And in that year also . . .', which appear appended to some of the chapters of the account of Murād II's reign.[1] H. Inalcık has now recognized[2] that entries of this type derive from a chronological list close to those in the almanacs.

Neshrī's first clear borrowing appears in his long chapter on Bāyezīd I's campaigns in Karaman and Eastern Anatolia, where, in an aside, he comments (*Mz* 87, 9/*Ank* 320, 5): 'Before this [i.e. before Bāyezīd's expulsion of Ḳāḍī Burhāneddīn] there had been a battle (*vāḳiʿa*) between Bāyezīd and Ḳāḍī Burhāneddīn at a place called Kırk-Dilim'. This battle is not mentioned in 'Āpz's History, nor was it (to judge from O.A.) in Neshrī's other main source;[3] but in the lists of the two latest almanacs, those for 856 and 858, appears the entry:[4] 'And since the battle (*vāḳiʿa*) at Kırk-Dilim between Ḳāḍī Burhāneddīn and Yıldırım Bāyezīd Khān it is 57/59 years' (i.e. the battle occurred in A.H. 799).[5] Five entries which Neshrī makes for the reign of Meḥemmed I agree almost verbatim with entries in these two lists, but with a consistent discrepancy of one year between the Hijra years recorded by Neshrī and the Hijra years to be calculated from the lists;[6] hence Neshrī's

[1] *Quellenproblem*, 115 f.

[2] H. Inalcık, *Fatih devri*, 23.

[3] Bāyezīd's capture of Kırk Dilim (north of Çorum) and his defeat shortly afterwards are described in 'Azīz b. Ardashīr's *Bazm u razm*, Istanbul 1928, 403 ff.

[4] This and the other sections of these lists which reflect the source used by Neshrī are quoted in Appendix III, pp. 76–80, below.

[5] Neshrī, relating events which he dates (after his second source, cf. O.A. 38*r*) to 794, ignores this date: no doubt he realized that for such an early reign the figures of his list were unreliable.

[6] See the concordance, p. 65: whereas the lists give [818–20], [822–3], Neshrī has 817–9, 821–2.

source, though very close in text to these two lists, was not identical with either. In Neshrī's eleven main borrowings for the reign of Murād II, however, his dates and the dates implied by the lists do in nine cases agree.[1] In taking over these entries Neshrī has incorporated into his History well over half of the Ottoman section of the latest lists.

One important detail in Neshrī's History may also be traced back to this source: he, almost alone of the fifteenth-century historians,[2] recognizes that the pretender Muṣṭafā who challenged Murād II's succession to the throne was indeed an Ottoman prince, substituting, for 'Āpz's phrase (*'Āpz* 86, 2) 'a pretender who claimed to be the son of Bāyezīd', 'Muṣṭafā Beg the son of Yıldırım Khān' (*Mz* 149, 6/*Ank* 556, 7). This is precisely the expression by which the lists refer to him.

To make a detailed analysis of Neshrī's method of combining his sources would be premature, with the text of O.A. and the closely-related History of Rūḥī still unpublished. The concordance given in Appendix I (pp. 58–69, below), however, shows in outline how Neshrī has had recourse to the three works he used for his Ottoman *ṭabaḳa*. He has taken over practically the whole of 'Āpz's History, the bulk of what O.A. indicates as standing in his second source, and more than half of his chronological list.

In general he is content—as indeed is to be expected of the author of a vast world-history—to reproduce his sources with little modification. As a universal historian, however, he is very careful in his first chapters on the Ottomans to fit the imprecise and legendary stories of their origins into the context of contemporary Islamic history. He is at pains to omit or make impersonal 'Āpz's autobiographical references;[3] he usually omits his verses—which to Neshrī's taste must have been very primitive—but occasionally recasts them into prose;[4] the 'questions and answers' characteristic of 'Āpz's dramatic style are paraphrased into

[1] See the concordance, p. 66: the exceptions are that the lists group under [824] and [833] events which Neshrī distributes between 824 and 825, and 832 and 833.

[2] The other exception is Enverī, see *Düsturnamei Enveri*, ed. M. Halil [Yınanç], Istanbul, 1928, 92.

[3] There is one crucial exception, see pp. 21–23, below.

[4] The exceptions are when 'Āpz's verses contain factual detail, e.g. *Mz* 38, 9–12; 46, 9; 97, 3–4 (cf. *'Āpz* 28, 1–5; 40, 11–14; 71, 23–25 respectively).

narrative; and 'Āpz's criticisms of the Čandarlı family are usually omitted.[1] But otherwise 'Āpz's style and vocabulary are faithfully reproduced.[2] The material from the second source, often at variance with 'Āpz's account, is very carefully woven in: Neshrī implies in his introduction that his aim is to bring together disparate sources and harmonize their chronologies. Only here and there is a logical discrepancy to be detected: Bāyezīd I's son Ertoghrul is said (*Mz* 98, 6/*Ank* 364, 4, probably following the second source) to have been killed in the campaign against Ḳāḍī Burhāneddīn, but he appears, still alive, some time after that campaign had taken place, according to Neshrī's readjusted chronology (*Mz* 92, 21/*Ank* 338, 15, following *'Āpz* 66, 26); again, the sack of Tokat by the Ak-koyunlu in 877/1472 is related twice, firstly (*Mz* 207, 9 ff./*Ank* 798, 1 ff.) after 'Āpz (§ 149), and again (*Mz* 208, 11 ff./*Ank* 802, 13 ff.) after the second source (cf. O.A. fols. 154^{v}–155^{r}).

When Neshrī's text is compared with his written sources and the contribution of his three informants is allowed for,[3] the residuum, the insertions he may be presumed to have made from his own knowledge, is found to be very small indeed.[4] There are a few chronograms and lines of verse. Otherwise, and perhaps significantly, these insertions nearly all concern Karaman and Bursa. Five chapters on events in Karaman (those beginning at *Mz* 200, 4; 202, 7; 205, 6; 206, 19; 207, 9/*Ank* 770, 13; 778, 8; 790, 3; 796, 1; 798, 1) contain expansions, apparently made by Neshrī himself, on the ruling family, its quarrels, and the course of the campaigns. As for Bursa, we find recorded an alternative story concerning the Ottoman capture of the town and 'Os̱mān's death (*Mz* 40, 10 ff./*Ank* 144, 4 ff.); there are details in the chapter on

[1] e.g. Neshrī omits at *Mz* 90, 7; 91, 2; 180, 3, the polemics at *'Āpz* 61, 19 ff.; 63, 13 ff.; 131, 18 ff. respectively.

[2] In just one case, 'Āpz's story of the capture of Aydos (§§ 26–27), does Neshrī make fundamental changes; see P. Wittek, 'The taking of Aydos castle: a ghāzī legend and its transformation', to be published in a forthcoming volume of studies in honour of Sir Hamilton Gibb.

[3] For Mevlānā Ayās and Meḥ. b. Ḳuṭbeddīn see p. 2, n. 2, above. Turakhān Beg-oghlu 'Omer Beg, who was taken prisoner by Uzun Ḥasan, is named as the authority for the chapter beginning at *Mz* 210, 5/*Ank* 810, 11; he probably supplied also extra details found in the other chapters on the Terjan campaign.

[4] This discussion concerns only the material found in Mz, the earlier recension (see Ch. IV), which lacks several further additions made in the later recension (Ch. VI).

Murād I's character and works (*Mz* 83, 10/*Ank* 306, 7) and in that on the siege by the Karaman-oghlu in 816/1413 (*Mz* 141, 11/*Ank* 516, 13) which sound like local traditions; and some sidelights on Maḥmūd Pasha's stay there (*Mz* 191, 10–13/*Ank* 742, 9–12) and on Jem's occupation of the district (*Mz* 220, 9 ff., 221, 16 ff.) seem to come from an eyewitness. These details lend weight to Laṭīfī's statement that Neshrī was a native of Karaman and to the late tradition, by itself less than convincing, that Neshrī lived in Bursa.

IV

THE CODEX MENZEL

THE earliest known manuscript of Neshrī's History is that acquired in 1929 in Kastamuni by Th. Menzel, after whom it is now named. Upon his death in 1939, the publication of the materials he left was entrusted by the German Academy to F. Taeschner, who in 1951 issued a facsimile from photocopies (the manuscript itself was destroyed towards the end of the Second World War).

The colophon of Mz states that it was completed 'between the noon and afternoon prayers'[1] on Tuesday, 25 Rebīʿ II 898 = 12 Feb. 1493 (Era 15). It is written in a rapid cursive neskh—the hand not of a professional copyist but of a scholar. One or two leaves have been lost from the beginning of the manuscript and two separate leaves from the body of the text.

Taeschner showed that Mz represents a distinct recension of the text, earlier than that to which the manuscripts used for *Ank* belong.[2] His arguments were: (1) the absence in Mz of various passages found in the other manuscripts, one of which at least,[3] interrupting as it does the narrative in Mz, must represent an interpolation; (2) the more archaic style and vocabulary of Mz as against the other manuscripts, whose text has undergone a stylistic revision; (3) the several cases where Mz alone among the manuscripts reproduces a proper name correctly; and (4) the several cases where Mz's readings alone give good sense, while the other manuscripts have readings which either are meaningless or reveal that the text has been misinterpreted. So numerous indeed are the corruptions in the later, revised, recension (as attested by the consensus of all the manuscripts except Mz) that Taeschner was

[1] *'bayna 'l-ṣalātayn'*: this term is explained in H. Fleischer and F. Delitzsch, *Catalogus librorum manuscriptorum qui in Bibl. senat. civit. Lipsiensis asservantur*, Grimae, 1838, 422.

[2] *Mn* (*Einl.*), 3–13.

[3] *Ank* 134, 14–19, a passage on the settlement of Muslims in the newly-conquered Bursa, which interrupts *Mz* 39, 21: 'nobody contests that Bursa was conquered in that year, | but what is contested is . . . .' For this and other interpolations in the later recension see Ch. VI.

doubtful whether the revision is to be attributed to Neshrī himself; the reviser might even, he suggested, have been working after Neshrī's death.

Taeschner's list of examples, taken from the first few pages of the text, which show Mz alone reproducing a proper name correctly and Mz's readings clearly giving better sense, can be considerably extended.[1] But the conclusive proof of the priority of Mz emerges from later pages, where its text can be compared with Neshrī's known sources.

To take 'Āpz first. The most illuminating variant occurs in Neshrī's re-casting of part of *'Āpz* § 113 (a very confused chapter), the description of an expedition led by Isḥāḳ Beg in the middle of Murād II's reign, in which 'Āpz himself had taken part. 'Āpz says (114, 19 ff.):

اول زمان‌ده کرمیان سنجاغی بکی تمورتاش اوغلی اومور بکك
اوغلی عثمان جلبیدیکم اول وارنه اوغرشنده شهید اولدی |[a] فقیر اول
زمانده اسکوبه اسحاق بکله کلمشیدم کاه کاه بو ماجرالرده بله بولنوردم
وبر دفعه دخی اسحاق بکك اوغلی پاشا بکله وقلججی طوغانیله
حراملغه بله کتمشدم |[b] بر کون لشکر اچنده بر غوغا بلوردی اسحاق
بك همان ات ارقاسنه سوار اولدی جمیعی غازلر دخی ات ارقسنه کلدلر
ناکاه کردك (*c*) قارشودن بر الای کفار چقه‌کلدی وانلرك اردندن بر
نچه الای دخی کلدی کفار یایه‌سن اوکنه طوتمش واتلوسن اردنه
طوتمش قپقاره پوس اولوب همان اوزروموزه (*d*) یورودی

... At that time the beg of the sanjak of Germiyān was 'Osmān Čelebi son of Umur Beg son of Timurtash (who was killed in the battle of

[1] For proper names, see also *Mz* 10, 6: '*Muslim b. Ḳuraysh al-'Uḳaylī*' (deformed at *Mn* 10, 14, *Ank* 26, 11); *Mz* 11, 21: '*veled-i aṣgharı Ghiyāṣ al-Dīn*' (*veled* is lacking, with consequent confusion, at *Mn* 12, 19, *Ank* 32, 5); *Mz* 12, 10 gives the names of Yaghıbasan and his three sons correctly, cf. Ibn Bībī (Erzi), 76, 16 (corrupted at *Mn* 13, 11, *Ank* 32, 17); *Mz* 17, 8: 'from the Crimea, the land of the Khazars', cf. Ibn Bībī (Erzi), 735 (but 'to Khwarezm', *Mn* 20, 9, *Ank* 48, 12). For examples of better sense see also *Mz* 8, 18, a line on the origin of the Seljuks which has been lost by haplography at *Mn* 8, 16, *Ank* 22, 4; *Mz* 9, 21: 'pursued him to Ṭūs [*Ṭūsa-dak*]' (but 'made him prisoner [*tutsak*]', *Mn* 10, 6, *Ank* 26, 2); *Mz* 18, 2: 'the fortress in the pass [*dervendi*] of Sögüt' (but 'Sögüt and its seven [*-dür ve yedi*] fortresses', *Mn* 21, 7, *Ank* 50, 12).

Varna). [a] I had at that time returned to Üsküb with Isḥāḳ Beg, and from time to time was present on these enterprises. On one occasion I had gone out on a raid in company with Isḥāḳ Beg's son Pasha Beg and Kılıččı Doghan. [b] One day a tumult was heard among the troops. Isḥāḳ Beg immediately mounted his horse and all the ghāzīs mounted too. All of a sudden we saw that (*c*) an enemy company had appeared in the path and that behind them many more companies had come up. With their infantry in front and their cavalry in the rear they immediately advanced upon us (*d*) in a dense black cloud.

This passage is reproduced in Mz (168, 8 ff.) as follows:

اول زمانده کرمیان سنجاغی بکی تمورتاش اوغلی اسور بك اوغلی
عثمان جلبیدی کم صکره وارنه غزاسنده شهید اولدی [a] القصه [b] بر
کون لشکر اچنده بر غوغا بلوردی اسحاق بك همان‌دم آت ارقاسنه
کلدی جمیع لشکر دخی آتلندی نا کاه (*c*) قرشودن بر آلای کافر چقه‌کلب
ارتلرندن بر نچه آلای دخی کلدی یایالرن ایلینه طوتمش اتلوسی
اردنه طورمش قبقره بوس اولب دخی ازرمزه (*d*) یوردی

. . . At that time the beg of the sanjak of Germiyān was ʿOs̲mān Čelebi, son of Umur Beg, son of Timurtash (who was killed later in the ghazā of Varna). [a] To be brief: [b] One day a tumult was heard among the troops. Isḥāḳ Beg immediately mounted his horse and all the troops mounted too. All of a sudden (*c*) an enemy company appeared in the path and behind them many more companies came up. With their infantry in front and their cavalry remaining in the rear they advanced upon us (*d*) in a dense black cloud.

Thus Neshrī follows ʿĀpz closely as far as (*a*). ʿĀpz then digresses to explain that he and his patron Isḥāḳ Beg had already returned to Üsküb (from the Pilgrimage) and refers to other forays in which he had partaken (*a–b*); he returns to his main theme to relate—in the first person plural—an incident which occurred on that expedition. Neshrī omits the whole of (*a–b*), for it is his practice to drop (as here) or to make impersonal the autobiographical references in ʿĀpz's text; the word *al-ḳiṣṣa*, here substituted, is his normal device when skipping part of his source or when switching from one source to another. He then reproduces the gist of ʿĀpz's story, suppressing the first-person verb *gördük* (*c*), but failing to modify the other first-person reference *üzerimize* (*d*). That this latter was due to oversight appears from the other manuscripts: *Mn* 246,

10, reads, for *üzerimize*, *ghāzīler üzerine*, and *Ank* 628, 8 (no variants listed!) omits the word, so that here too the personal reference has been made impersonal. Mz, here standing closer to 'Āpz than any other manuscript, is proved to represent an earlier recension. (Furthermore, it is seen that the reviser who removed from the text the first-person reference *üzerimize* shared Neshrī's concern to make 'Āpz's autobiographical references impersonal: here, in other words, is a first indication that the reviser might have been Neshrī himself. To this and other 'revisions' we return in Ch. VI.)

These further examples show how comparison with 'Āpz demonstrates that Mz presents the earlier and good reading, while the later recension, as attested by *Mn* and *Ank*, is corrupt. The later recension has here and there lost words by haplography:

1. *'Āpz* 67, 9, *Mz* 93, 3: '[Bāyezīd I took] . . . Behisni from the Türkmens'; these words have been lost at *Mn* 143, 8, *Ank* 340, 3.
2. *'Āpz* 113, 13, *Mz* 167, 15: 'a prisoner capable of looking after horses was sold for 150 akčes'; dropped at *Mn* 245, 10, *Ank* 626, 2.
3. *'Āpz* 114, 10: 'they imprisoned Drakula at Gelibolu; they imprisoned his two sons at Egrigöz in Germiyan; they imprisoned Vılk-oghlu's two sons at Tokat'; *Mz* 168, 3, has only the first and second clauses (Neshrī's eye having jumped from the second *ḥabsetdiler* in 'Āpz to the third), and *Mn* 245, 18, *Ank* 626, 14, owing to a further similar omission, have only the first clause.
4. *'Āpz* 150, 13, *Mz* 192, 14 have a line lost in *Mn* 276, 2, *Ank* 746, 6.

Elsewhere the later recension has a misreading of a proper name:

5. *'Āpz* 58, 22: *'Edreneye'*; *Mz* 84, 11: *'Edrenede'*; but *Mn* 131, 16, *Ank* 310, 19: *'devrinde'*.
6. *'Āpz* 79, 24: *'Sulṭān Meḥemmedüŋ oghlı Sulṭān Murād'*, *Mz* 145, 7: *'Murād ibn Meḥemmed Khān'*; but *Mn* 216, 11, *Ank* 540, 5: *'Sulṭān Meḥemmed'*.
7. *'Āpz* 88, 7, *Mz* 151, 6: *'Lapsakuya'*; but *Mn* 224, 13, *Ank* 564, 2: *'iskeleye'*.
8. *'Āpz* 94, 22, *Mz* 155, 2: *'Isḥāḳ Begüŋ'*; but *Mn* 230, 2: *'sanjak begüŋ,'* and *Ank* 580, 7: *'uj sanjaghı beginüŋ'*.

Comparison with Neshrī's other main source, as represented by O.A., gives the same results:

9. O.A. fol. 79^{v} relates how Meḥemmed Čelebi, preparing to repel Emīr Suleymān's invasion of Anatolia, summoned his troops: '*ve Toyran* [a] *Bege mektūb gönderdi ki Toyran Beg karındashum kerem ve lutf edüb bize yoldashlık edesiz deyü elči gönderijek Toyran* [b] *Beg dakhi yigitlerin ve bahādurların jemʿ edüb . . .*'; *Mz* 123, 10 has the whole sentence, but in *Mn* 185, 12 and *Ank* 452, 7 the words *a–b* have been dropped by haplography.
10. O.A. fol. 81^{v} describes how the commander at Ankara, besieged by Emīr Suleymān, sent an appeal for help to Meḥemmed by the hand of '*Eyne Khoja ve Bulghur Agha laḳablu bir kimesne*'; this phrase is reproduced in *Mz* 124, 20 (and 125, 3); but in *Mn* 187, 9 and 14, and *Ank* 456, 13 and 19, 'Eyne Khoja whose *laḳab* was Bulghur Agha' has become two people 'Eyne Khoja' and 'Bulghur Agha'.
11. O.A. fol. 97^{r} relates how Meḥemmed, defeated by Mūsā Čelebi at Injügez, made a campaign against Izmir and returned to Amasya; it proceeds: '*andan yene Rumiline gečüb karındashı Mūsā Beg birle yene durushub jenk etmek hevesi ghālib olub . . .*'; this is reproduced at *Mz* 136, 20; but in *Mn* 204, 11, *Ank* 500, 11, for اتمك هوسی there appears ایتدی موسی جلبی. The sense is now completely different: it is not Meḥemmed's eagerness (*heves*) to fight which overcomes him, but Mūsā (patently a misreading موسی / هوسی) himself; *Mn* adds that Meḥemmed, after this entirely mythical defeat, fled to Brusa, and *Ank* has still more circumstantial detail before embarking on the decisive campaign against Mūsā, now the third expedition.

Comparison with the chronological lists also provides one example:

12. The lists (see p. 78, below, l. 6) and *Mz* 162, 21 have the words '*baʿżı Shāma*', lost at *Mn* 239, 13 and *Ank* 610, 5.

At the same time such comparison proves the existence in the text of Mz of one or two defects more serious than the slips mentioned by Taeschner;[1] thus:

[1] *Mn* (*Einl.*), 5 and 11.

13. *Mz* 87, 13 lacks, by haplography, the words '*Ḳāḍī Burhāneddīn* [*oghlını Dul-Ḳādir oghlı Naṣreddīn Bege gönderdiler zīrā Ḳāḍī Burhāneddīn*] *Dul-Ḳādir oghlına*...', found at *Mn* 135, 18, *Ank* 320, 11, and justified by '*Āpz* 66, 6.
14. *Mz* 149, 14 lacks, also by haplography, words found at *Mn* 222, 8, *Ank* 558, 1, and justified by '*Āpz* 86, 12.

Mz is not then a perfect text and cannot, as Taeschner points out,[1] have served as exemplar for the remaining manuscripts. Nevertheless the comparison shows that it is an exceedingly good text, and that it stands in an intermediate position between the sources and the remaining manuscripts.

Besides these points of detail however, there is one major difference between the text of Mz and the common text of the later recension, namely their arrangement of the chapters of 'Os̱mān Ghāzī's reign.[2] In Mz the sequence of the first chapters of this section is:

(i)	*Mz* 23, 4–16	'The beginning of the Ottoman State'
(ii)	*Mz* 23, 16–24, 3	The story of Ertoghrul and the Koran
(iii)	*Mz* 24, 3–7	'Os̱mān succeeds Ertoghrul (appended to (ii) without a new heading)
(iv)	*Mz* 24, 7–25, 3	'Os̱mān marries Mal-khātūn
(v)	*Mz* 25, 3–7	Death of Ertoghrul

None of these chapters depends on 'Āpz, but from here onwards Neshrī broadly reproduces '*Āpz* §§ 3–22, with some slight transpositions and a few additions from his second source. Still mainly following 'Āpz, Mz then proceeds:

(*a*)	*Mz* 38, 12–40, 5	Capture of Brusa	= '*Āpz* § 23
(*b*)	*Mz* 40, 5–10	'Os̱mān's testament	= '*Āpz* § 24
(*c*)	*Mz* 40, 10–15	Alternative account of 'Os̱mān's death (tradition? see pp. 18–19, above)	
(*d*)	*Mz* 40, 15–41, 9	Exploits of the ghāzīs	= '*Āpz* § 25
(*e*)	*Mz* 41, 9–42, 8	Capture of Aydos	= '*Āpz* § 26
(*f*)	*Mz* 42, 9–13	and its sequel	= '*Āpz* § 27
(*g*)	*Mz* 42, 14–15	'Character' of 'Os̱mān	= '*Āpz* p. 193, 10
(*h*)	*Mz* 42, 15–19	Death of 'Os̱mān	= '*Āpz* § 28

[1] *Mn* (*Einl.*), 11.

[2] Taeschner discusses this question at *Mn* (*Einl.*), 7; he points out that Mz's order seems to be the older, but does not adduce the proof, which emerges from comparison with the text of 'Āpz.

In the later recension the sequence of the chapters in the first block (*Mn* 27–31, *Ank* 70–78) is: (i), (iii), (*g*), (ii), (iv), (v), and in the second block (*Mn–Pa* 55–64, *Ank* 128–146): (*a*), (*d*), (*e*), (*f*), (*h*), (*c*), (*b*). There is one significant revision of the text: in *Mz*, (ii) describes how Ertoghrul, staying in the house of a holy man, stood all night in respect before a copy of the Koran;[1] in the later recension the hero is not Ertoghrul but ʿOsmān Ghāzī (*Mn* 29, 1, *Ank* 72, 13). Mz's order cannot be an accidental disarrangement by a copyist, for in Mz the second block follows very closely ʿĀpz's sequence of chapters, while the later recension departs from ʿĀpz's order; Mz therefore has the original order and the later recension a revised order.

The explanation for the rearrangement in the first block is probably to be found in the reviser's decision to make ʿOsmān, and not Ertoghrul, the hero of the Koran story (ii), which must therefore be postponed a little. (iii), which begins with the words '*ve bi'l-jümle Ertoghrul* . . .', no longer follows (ii) naturally, but fits very well onto the closing words of (i), a 'character' of Ertoghrul. The character of ʿOsmān is now brought in, (*g*), perhaps to compare his character with that of Ertoghrul and to provide a bridge to the Koran story (ii), an illustration of ʿOsmān's piety. The reviser then returns to Mz's order for (iv) and (v).

The key to the rearrangement in the second block is the Arabic sentence هذا مؤخر من ورقين مربوط بآخر, which appears, *only in Mz*, at the end of (*b*). It seems to mean 'This is to be postponed a couple of pages, attached to the end',[2] i.e. appended to (*h*), which is in Mz the last chapter of ʿOsmān's reign; and this is precisely where (*b*) and (*c*) do appear, though transposed, in the later recension. The reason for the rearrangement is also fairly clear: having followed ʿĀpz's order to the end of (*b*), Neshrī recollects another account of ʿOsmān's death (probably Bursa tradition) which seems to him more reliable (*aṣaḥḥ*, *Mz* 40, 10) than ʿĀpz's; he finds also that ʿĀpz proceeds with three chapters (§§ 25–27) on the exploits of other warriors which are interposed unnaturally between the accounts of ʿOsmān's testament (§ 24) and of his death (§ 28). He

[1] Neshrī is here following his second source: the passage is lost in O.A. but is reproduced, with Ertoghrul as the hero, by Rūḥī (see *Mitt. z. Osm. Gesch.* ii. 131).

[2] Interpreting the last word as *bi-'ākhir*, although the writer perhaps intended *bi-'ākhar*, 'to another [section]', 'elsewhere'.

therefore makes this Arabic note as a reminder when revising to move to the end (*b*), which he has just written, and (*c*), which he now proceeds to write. Given that Mz presents the chapters in an order closer to that of the source, the order which a compiler would naturally follow at a first writing, the note can have been made only by Neshrī himself: *hence Mz here reproduces Neshrī's draft.*[1]

In the light of this, the hand of the compiler at work can be detected at two other points in Mz (and in no other manuscript):

15. In describing how Isfendiyār made over part of his territories to Meḥemmed I, ʿĀpz makes him say (79, 14):

وبن خونکاره وررین قاسمه ورمزین ددی انو کیچونکم بدبختدر
ددی خونکار داخی |[a] کرو قاسمه |[b] وردی

This is reproduced in Mz (145, 4) with a small addition:

بن بونلری خونکارك کندوسنه وردم قاسمه ورمسون که
بدبختدر خونکاره دیدلر قبول ایدب ینه قاسمه |[c] ایلغاز طاغنی
حدیله تعیین ایدب |[d] ینه قاسم بکه صدقه اتدی

The detail that the Ilghāz mountains were made the frontier (*c–d*) is interpolated by Neshrī, who has found it in his second source (it appears in O.A., fol. 105ᵛ). But why do the superfluous words *yine Ḳāsime* appear just before it? Evidently because Neshrī had followed ʿĀpz *as far as* (*b*) before realizing that the detail on the frontier must be added; having inserted it he returns to the text of ʿĀpz, *resuming from* (*a*), and forgetting to strike out the now redundant *yine Ḳāsime*. (In the later recension, which has also undergone some stylistic revision, the *Ḳāsime* has been removed, cf. *Mn* 216, 9, *Ank* 540, 1.)

16. In the bottom margin of *Mz* 164 is written, in the same hand as the text, a note recording the death of Shemseddīn Fenārī in 838 with a verse in Persian in his praise. In *Mn* 242, 4 the death is recorded at the equivalent point, but now incorporated in the text, in fewer words and without the verse; in *Ank* 616, 10, presumably here following MS. W,

[1] The suggestion that Mz might be a draft version of the text was made, but not pursued, by F. Taeschner, *Mn* (*Einl.*), 12.

the note on the death is lacking altogether. Whatever the silence of the other manuscripts may imply,[1] Mn's reading proves that the note was intended to belong to the text; so that Mz, which has it as an afterthought in the margin, is shown again to represent the draft.

These features of Mz raise a further question. Is Mz a transcript of Neshrī's autograph draft, whose copyist has reproduced the Arabic note and the marginal entry exactly as he found them, or might Mz be the autograph draft itself? There are two indications that this might be so:

17. Describing Murād I's capture of Mesini in Thrace, 'Āpz writes (48, 11):

اندن مسنی حصارنه واردلر تکوری قرشو کلدی |[a] بر اوغلنی بله
کاتردی حصارنك کلیدین دخی کتوردی سلطان مراد غازی خان
دخی واردی حصارك اوزرنه قوندی تکوری دخی مبالغه |[b] پشکشلر
چکدی خان دخی جمیعسنی غازلره وردی

For this Mz (52, 21) has only:

اندن مسنی حصارنه واردلر تکوری سلطان مراده قرشو وارب
(53) پیش کشلر چکدی خان دخی جمیعسن غازیلره قسمت اتدی

and substantially the same briefer account is found in the later recension (*Mn* 80, 15, *Ank* 192, 15, but with the misreading حسنی). Thus in all manuscripts of Neshrī the words (*a–b*) of 'Āpz have been dropped, either intentionally or by accident. There is nothing in the text to suggest an intentional omission: Neshrī departs from 'Āpz only when he prefers the account of another source or when he is censoring the text for identifiable reasons. Nor does the content of the text provide any clue to explain an accidental omission —by haplography, for example, as in passages 13 and 14 above. But on the hypothesis that Mz is the autograph an explanation can be found: the omission occurs precisely at the point where the writer of Mz began a new page, and so might have had his attention distracted.

[1] Revision? The death of the same Shemseddīn Fenārī has in fact been noted before this, under the year 832, at *Mz* 162, 16, *Ank* 608, 17, there following the chronological list (see p. 77, items for [833]).

18. *Mz* 180, 6 ff. reads:

سلطان محمّد ایتدی لالا بو یل استانبولی یایلرن |[a] عساکر
عظیمه جمع ایدب الحاصل یریوب (?) |[b] چون که خونکار استانبوله
متوجه اولدی تکفوری کرلوقه نام کافر وزیرن الجلکله کندرب
امان دیلدی خونکار التفات اتمدی |[c] الحاصل یوریب اسبابی احضار
ایدب عساکر عظیمه جمع ایدب . . .

The words (*a*–*b*) are deleted, but reappear, slightly paraphrased, after (*c*). As far as (*a*) Neshrī is following ʿĀpz (132, 5); (*b*–*c*) is taken from the second source (cf. O.A. fol. 127^{r}, 4); the words following (*c*) are an abridgement of the second source (cf. O.A. fol. 127^{r}, 8), until at *Mz* 180, 10 Neshrī returns to ʿĀpz (132, 6). Here, as in passage 15 above, we see Neshrī hesitating as he harmonizes his sources: having begun, at (*a*), to paraphrase his second source, he decides to borrow from it at an earlier point, deletes what he has written and inserts (*b*–*c*). He then continues with a slightly different paraphrase of what he had begun to write at (*a*).[1] A copyist, however punctilious, does not trouble to reproduce from his model a deletion: the pen that wrote these lines of Mz in this form must be Neshrī's.

At first sight the hypothesis that Mz is an autograph seems to be excluded because of the presence in it of inferior readings: most of these, it is true, are simple slips which can be immediately corrected, but among them are some more serious omissions (passages 13 and 14, for example) where the sense is distorted. But if we make the assumptions—for which, as will appear, there is evidence—that the revised text was made by Neshrī himself and that in preparing it he checked his earlier text by going back to his sources, the objection loses its force. That Mz might be the autograph is suggested also by the scholarly hand in which it is written and by its exceptionally early date, 898/1493—the date, on this hypothesis, of composition.[2]

[1] The words (*a*–*b*) cannot be a copyist's 'anticipation', for the paraphrase after (*c*) is differently worded. At *Mn* 260, 12, *Ank* 688, 14 the whole passage has been slightly recast and smoothed out.

[2] The manuscript described by Smirnov (see above, p. 6, n. 1), which may be Neshrī's autograph for the *ṭabaḳa* on the ʿAbbāsids, is written in a more

Autograph or not, Mz represents a draft. But of which text? Neshrī wrote first his Universal History, the *Jihān-numā*, in six sections, and later separated off the sixth section to stand as an independent work, the 'History of the Oghuzian Turks'. The *Jihān-numā*, Neshrī tells us, was completed to the stage of the fair copy (*Ank* 6, 11); so that if Mz derives from the *Jihān-numā*, a finished work, it is difficult to account for the evidences of uncertainty and lack of final revision which it presents. But that Mz should be anterior to the *Jihān-numā*, should be, in other words, the draft for its sixth section, fits the facts very well. We thus have the sequence:

1. Draft for section six of the *Jihān-numā* (represented by Mz).
2. Fair copy version of section six of the *Jihān-numā* (no manuscript extant).
3. The independent 'History of the Oghuzian Turks' (manuscripts of the later recension).[1]

elegant and careful hand than Mz, but it is not impossible that the two were written by the same man: a man of letters might write in more than one style.

[1] This question would not require discussion if the first pages of Mz had survived, for section six of the *Jihān-numā* must have begun immediately with the table of contents (*Ank* 6, 15–19), whereas the 'History of the Oghuzian Turks' begins with an introduction, either newly-written for it or transferred from the beginning of the *Jihān-numā* (p. 7, above); but the defective text of Mz begins only at a point well into the first *ṭabaḳa*, and it is now impossible, as the manuscript is destroyed, to decide from the stitching how many leaves (two or one) have been lost, and hence whether the introduction figured in it or not.

V

THE CODEX HANIVALDANUS

LEUNCLAVIUS'S *Historiae musulmanae Turcorum de monumentis ipsorum exscriptae libri xviii*, Frankfurt, 1591, is mainly based on two texts: (i) the Codex Verantianus, a compilation in Italian translated from two recensions of the Anonymous Chronicles;[1] and (ii) the Codex Hanivaldanus, a compilation in Latin, made by the Court interpreter Murād[2] from various Turkish works for Count Philipp Haniwald, the secretary of the Imperial ambassador in Constantinople.[3]

[1] For the Codex Verantianus (Ver.), 'e Turcica lingua transcriptus in Italicam' (*H.M.* 115, 28), see P. Wittek's note in *Mitt. z. Osm. Gesch.* i, 1921–22, 11, and *Quellenproblem*, 140. Comparison of its text, as attested by *H.M.*, with the Anonymous Chronicles (*Anon.*) edited by F. Giese shows that it was a compilation from two recensions. It followed Type W_1 (i.e. the fuller text) almost to its end: *H.M.* 596, 48–604, 10 (certainly following Ver., see *H.M.* 593, 10–18) reproduces *Anon.* 118, 13–125, 10; it then followed the text of Type W_3, ending at the same point as Giese's MS. V[enedig]: *H.M.* 604, 11–618, 15 = *Anon.* 125, 7–133, 9, and *H.M.* 740, 15–800, 19 = *Anon.* 133, 10–151, 17.

[2] Murād was by birth a Hungarian; taken prisoner at the age of seventeen at the battle of Mohacs (1526), he embraced Islam and became, thanks to his knowledge of Latin and the favour of Rustem Pasha, one of the interpreters of the Porte. He composed, in Turkish and later in Latin, a missionary treatise *Taṣwiyat al-tawajjuh ilā 'l-ḥaḳḳ*, and in 967/1559–60 made a Turkish paraphrase of Cicero's *De Senectute*, commissioned by the Venetian bailo Marino de' Cavalli for presentation to Suleymān. Some time after 1576 he was dismissed from his post for addiction to wine. He then composed, perhaps in the hope of regaining favour, a trilingual (Turkish-Latin-Hungarian) hymn, and at about the same time, to earn money, made the translation for Haniwald (see F. Babinger, 'Der Pfortendolmetsch Murād und seine Schriften', in *Literaturdenkmäler aus Ungarns Türkenzeit*, Berlin and Leipzig, 1927, 33–54, and E. Rossi, 'Parafrasi turca del *de Senectute* . . .', *Rend. d. R. Acc. Naz. d. Lincei*, ser. 6, vol. xii, 1936, 680–756).

[3] Annexed (*adiunctum*, *H.M.* 222, 15) to Ver. was another work, also translated from Turkish, 'de variis astutiis et fraudibus Osmaneorum' (*H.M.* 306, 37), see *Quellenproblem*, 141. It is apparently to this work and not to the true 'Ver.' that Leunclavius is referring at *H.M.* 42, 15: 'in uno . . . Verantiano codice: cuius interpres fuisse videtur Graecus aliquis, linguae quidem Turcicae gnarus; sed Italicae, qua usus est in reddendis Turcorum commentariis, admodum rudis. Eos X libris distinctos, ipsemet ad initium codicis adnotavit scriptos Sultani Baiasitis II tempore, videlicet a centum plus minus annis' (whereas Ver. reached beyond the middle of the reign of Suleymān, see n. 1, above);

Hammer's assertion (*GOR*, I. xxxiv) that the latter reproduced the bulk of Neshrī's Ottoman History was followed up by P. Wittek, who, in his *Quellenproblem*, made a detailed study of the relationship between the texts.

The Codex Hanivaldanus (hereafter Han.) relied for most of its account of the reign of Meḥemmed II on an annalistic text very close to that of the Codex Verantianus (i.e. on one recension of the Anonymous Chronicles),[1] and for its account of the reigns of Bāyezīd II and Selīm I on a text, so far unidentified, which has no connexion with the text of Neshrī;[2] Neshrī's text is reflected only in the portion of Han. which described events from the rise of the Ottomans down to the rebuilding of Constantinople after its capture.[3]

On comparing this central block with the text of Neshrī's History as represented by the Vienna MS. (W), Wittek found that the Neshrī of W was not identical with the 'Neshrī' of Han.; even after variations in detail and minor omissions in Han., which might be ascribed to the carelessness of a copyist or of the translator, were left aside, the difficulty remained that W contained several whole episodes lacking in Han. He therefore postulated the existence of a compilation X (composed from the History of 'Āshiḳpashazāde

cf. *H.M.* 222, 12: 'Non semel vero iam ante diximus, historiae Verantianae commentarium quemdam adiunctum esse, qui varios astus et exempla perfidiae insignis contineat; quibus imperium Osmanicum a principio magnum illud ad culmen excrescere ceperit. Is liber ab interprete Graeco, Turcorum e lingua redditus fuit.' The Turkish original, probably a story book rather than a 'history', remains unidentified.

[1] *H.M.* 582, 5: 'Ad historiae seriem ut redeamus, quae deinceps propemodum eadem est in libris ambobus'; *H.M.* 583, 2–594, 4 = *Anon.* (Type W_1) 111, 19–116, 12. *H.M.* contains the substance of the later part of the 'Legendary History of Constantinople' (*H.M.* 32, 20– , cf. *Anon.* 100, 21–), and this appeared, as Leunclavius indicates, in Han. as well as in Ver., cf. *H.M.* 34, 42 'vel Affan, quod Murates begus posuit' (= *Anon.* 101, 25), 35, 15 'Ibni-Mulzeme, quod Murates nomen edidit' (= *Anon.* 102, 2). Murād (or an earlier redactor), after following his Neshrī text to the end of the chapter on Meḥemmed's foundations in Istanbul (*Mz* 182, 11/*Ank* 712, 13 = *H.M.* 582, 35), turned to *Anon.* for the 'Legendary History' and then continued, beyond *Anon.* 111, with the latter's historical account.

[2] *H.M.* 618, 19–739, 49. Han. ended with the account of the events of 925/1519.

[3] See the concordance in Appendix I. In several of the early passages Leunclavius in conflating the almost identical accounts of Ver. (= *Anon.*) and Han. (= Neshrī < 'Āpz < an early recension of *Anon.*, see p. xv, above). The first peculiarity of Neshrī's text reflected in *H.M.* is the conclusion of its genealogy of the Ottoman Sultans (*H.M.* 89, 48–90, 21): '. . . Diptacoi, Bulchas, Iaphet, Noa . . .', cf. *Mz* 19, 10/*Ank* 56, 2 (though *H.M.*'s genealogy conflates Neshrī's with that of *Anon.*).

and other sources) standing between the texts of 'Āpz and Neshrī: from X Han. derived, and to X Neshrī made the additions found in W (see the schema at p. 10, above).

With the facsimiles of Mz and Mn and the two volumes of *Ank* now available the question may be reconsidered.

Wittek gave three examples of minor discrepancies in content, where Han. lacked short sentences found in W. In two cases *Mz* has substantially the same readings as W, and Wittek's explanation stands, namely that the absence of the sentences in Han. represents losses in the transmission of the text.[1] In the third case, however, the account of the sons of Murād II, comparison with *Mz* suggests a different explanation.

The Latin text reads (*H.M.* 572, 1):'Nati Sultano Murati fuere filii sex, his ordine nominibus: Achmetes, Alis . . ., Muhametes in regno successor, Hasen sive Chasan, Urchan, et Cutzug Achmet, hoc est Achmetes minor, sive secundus, ex Isfendiaris begi filia prognatus. [a]| Is Amasiae diem suum obiit, et ibidem in monumento filiorum Sultani Muhametis primi, Sultani Baiasitis I filii, sepultus fuit . . .', and then proceeds to relate the deaths of 'Alī, Ḥasan, and Orkhān. For this W (quoted at *Quellenproblem*, 120, and cf. *Ank* 682, 1) has:

وسلطان مرادك التی اوغلی اولدی بری احمد بری علی بری محمّد
بری حسن بری اورخان وبری اسفندیار قزندن اولمشدی کوچجك
احمد |[b] درلردی وبو سرایده ایدی وبیوك احمد |[c] اماسیده ألدی انده |[d]
بایزید خان اولادی تربسنده دفن اتدلر

The absence of the words '*Sulṭān Meḥemmed ibn*' (= Sultani Muhametis primi . . . filii) at *d* is a minor accident, peculiar to W (see *Ank* apparatus) and without significance. More serious is the fact that the words (*b–c*) of W are not represented at all in *H.M.* (we expect to find them reflected at *a*), so that the sense of the passage is quite different: whereas W relates that 'young Aḥmed' survived his father and that the elder Aḥmed, predeceasing him, was buried at Amasya, in *H.M.* it is 'young Aḥmed' who is buried at Amasya and the death of the elder Aḥmed is not mentioned.

[1] *Quellenproblem*, 143: *H.M.* lacks, at 304, 55 and 555, 39, a few words found at *Mz* 83, 14/*Ank* 306, 12 and *Mz* 170, 7/*Ank* 634, 3 respectively.

In Mz however we read (178, 2):

سلطان مرادك الت اوغلى اولدى احمد على محمّد حسن اورخان بر دخى اسفنديار قزندن كوججك احمد اماسيه‌ده فوت اولب انده سلطان محمّد بن بايزيد خان اولادى تربه‌سنده دفن اتدلر

i.e. here too the words (*b–c*) of W are lacking, so that we have the reading—not necessarily corrupt[1]—which has produced the Latin of Han.

A little farther on Neshrī—now following, almost verbatim, 'Āpz—mentions Meḥemmed II's burial of his father at Bursa and his execution of the (unnamed) younger brother (*Mz* 178, 13, following *'Āpz* 130, 7):

همان‌دم اتاسنك ميتنى بورسيه كندرب اول كوججك قرنداشى كه اسفنديار قزندن كه واردى مقامنه كوندردى

The last two words, *makāmına gönderdi*, are, of course, 'Āpz's euphemism for 'put him to death'. The other Neshrī MSS. (except Mn, which lacks the sentence on the child[2]) reproduce this passage with a variant: they have (*Ank* 682, 13), instead of the euphemism *makāmına gönderdi*, the unequivocal *ḥakk raḥmetine ulashdırub*. This passage appears in *H.M.* as follows (572, 54): 'Secundum haec patris sui funus illico Burusam deduci, et monumento propter fratrem minorem, (Cutzug Mustapha dubio procul,

[1] W's reading appears at first sight excellent, and Mz's to be the result of a haplography. Nevertheless I believe that the text of *Mz* 178, 3 (see the spacing of the words in this ?autograph manuscript) is to be 'punctuated' thus: '. . . *Meḥemmed, Ḥasan, Orkhān, bir dakhi İsfendiyār kızından—küčüjek. Aḥmed Amasyada* . . .', '. . . and yet another (a baby) by the daughter of Isfendiyār', i.e. the young sixth son is not named, and 'Aḥmed' refers to the eldest son who did indeed die as governor of Amasya. *Mn* 258, 3 (no variant in *Ank*!) reads: '. . . *bir dakhi İsfendiyār kızından oldı küčük Aḥmed nām Amasyada* . . .'; i.e. *oldı* and *nām* have been interpolated into the Mz reading. W's reading I take to be an (unjustified) emendation, for I can find no evidence, beyond these readings of some Neshrī manuscripts, the *mis*translation in *H.M.*, and later sources depending on them, that the child was in fact named Aḥmed: O.A. lacks a chapter on Murād II's family, but Neshrī's second source must have given him the list of *five* sons (Aḥmed to Orkhān) and their fates found in Shukrullāh 118, 9–13, to which Neshrī appended ('—*bir dakhi*'), from *'Āpz* 130, 7, a sixth son, *unnamed* there, born by the Isfendiyār princess (and executed).

[2] *Mn* 258, 13. This (tactful?) omission supports Wittek's suggestion (p. 9, above) that Mn was written as a prince's textbook!

Muratis ipsius frater, intellegitur) ex Isfendiaris filia natum, inferri iussit.' This is clearly a mistranslation: the dragoman Murād has interpreted the second part of the sentence as referring not to the *death* of Meḥemmed II's young brother (who for him is already dead—at Amasya) but to the *türbe* of Murād II's young brother 'Küčük Muṣṭafā'.

This misunderstanding can hardly have arisen because the translator misinterpreted *ḥaḳḳ raḥmetine ulashdırub*, 'sent him to encounter God's mercy': he must have been using a text which read here *maḳāmına gönderdi* (monumento [!] . . . inferri)—another reading which is peculiar to Mz. Here is a first indication that the work lying behind Han. was not necessarily a pre-Neshrī compilation but might be a text of the recension represented by Mz.

Wittek's main objection to identifying Han.'s source as Neshrī's History was the presence in MS. W of several long passages which are lacking in Han. and hence appeared to be additions made by Neshrī to the earlier compilation X. This objection melts away, however, when we turn to Mz. The passages which Wittek cited (*Quellenproblem*, 143) are:

(*a*) W 37^{v} = *Ank* 116, 8: a skirmish outside Bursa.
Lacking at *H.M.* 158, 15 and at *Mz* 35, 4.
(*b*) W 58^{v} = *Ank* 186, 10: Orkhān's buildings at Bursa.
Lacking at *H.M.* 215, 23 and at *Mz* 51, 21.
(*c*) W 152^{v} = *Ank* 518, 18: a stratagem during a siege of Bursa.
Lacking at *H.M.* 469, 39 and at *Mz* 142, 1.
(*d*) W 166^{r} = *Ank* 568, 15: a story of Ilyās Beg.
Lacking at *H.M.* 526, 20 and at *Mz* 152, 19.
(*e*) W 167^{r} = *Ank* 572, 16: a story of Mezīd Beg.
Lacking at *H.M.* 527, 30 and at *Mz* 153, 13.
(*f*) W 188^{r} = *Ank* 650, 2: incidents during the battle of Varna.
Lacking at *H.M.* 562, 27 and at *Mz* 173, 9.
(*g*) W 189^{r} = *Ank* 652, 18: the head of the Hungarian king sent to Bursa.
Lacking at *H.M.* 563, 25 and at *Mz* 173, 17.[1]

[1] Wittek cited a further passage, W 47^{r}, 1 (= *Ank* 144, 4), the alternative account of 'Oṣmān's death. This, passage (*c*) in the discussion at p. 25 above, is lacking at *H.M.* 175, 5, its logical place according to the arrangement of the later recension, but it appears at *H.M.* 173, 29 (see p. 36, n. 3, below).

In each case Mz stands with Han. against W, which is seen to have received several interpolations,[1] so that on the criterion of W's additional passages we need no longer—now that Mz has come to light—hesitate to regard Han. as deriving from a text of Neshrī's History.

One distinctive characteristic of Mz, we have noticed (p. 26), is that it tells the Koran story of Ertoghrul, whereas in all manuscripts of the later recension the story is told of 'Osmān and the neighbouring chapters (the 'first block') are, apparently as a consequence, rearranged. In Han. too, we find, the hero of the story was Ertoghrul: 'Accidit aliquando . . . ut Ertogrul in itinere quodam . . .' (*H.M.* 105, 21); furthermore *H.M.*'s account follows exactly Mz's sequence for the neighbouring chapters.[2] (The chapters of the 'second block', however, do seem to have already undergone some rearrangement in Han.:[3] to the possible significance of this we shall return.)

This close connexion between the texts of Mz and Han. is further demonstrated when the latter's readings are compared for the passages cited (under the numbers used here) in the foregoing chapter:

2. Han. read (*H.M.* 551, 49), with Mz: *Mancipium quoque masculum, curandis equis idoneum, aspris CL distractum fuit.*
3. Han. read (*H.M.* 552, 22), with Mz: *filii capti Germeanensem deducti sunt in regionem, et in arce custoditi, quam Egrigios Turci nominant.*
5. Han. read (*H.M.* 315, 43), with Mz: *Hadrianopolim.*
6. Han. read (*H.M.* 476, 1), with Mz: *Muhametis Chanis filium Muratem.*
7. Han. read (*H.M.* 489, 9), with Mz: *Lepseke.*

[1] See Ch. VI. The apparatus of *Ank* indicates that (*b*) and (*c*) were in the archetype α, the rest were introduced in the hyparchetype γ.

[2] See the Concordance, Appendix I. The interruption at *H.M.* 106, 9–107, 14, another story of the dream of Ertoghrul, must be from Ver. (it reproduces *Anon.* 6, 16–7, 6), and that at *H.M.* 110, 53–111, 10 is comment by Leunclavius.

[3] Leunclavius has evidently rearranged his material, splitting some chapters, in harmonizing Han. and Ver., and has very logically moved (*d*) (*e*) (*f*) forward into the section on Orkhān; in consequence the material of the 'second block' appears (see Concordance) in this order: a_1 [Ver.] a_2 c_1 a_3 h c_2(?) b g, certainly closer to the later recension's order than to Mz's. That (*g*) is still in the 'second block' is to be expected: its transference to the first block was necessitated by the rearrangement of the latter, and in Han. that had not yet occurred.

9. Han. read (*H.M.* 420, 48), with Mz: . . . *significatum per internuntium fuit, ut fratri suo . . . copias auxiliares adduceret. Mox Doioran . . .*
10. Han. read (*H.M.* 423, 43), with Mz: *Eini cuidam Hozzae, qui cognomine Bulgur Aga vocabatur.*
11. Han. read (*H.M.* 452, 31), with Mz: *Hinc rursus in Europaeam Rumiliam statuit transmittendum, et repetito cum fratre Musa proelio pugnandum*, without the additions found in Mn and *Ank*.
12. Han. read (*H.M.* 544, 16), with Mz: *Plerique Damascum.*
16. Han. recorded (*H.M.* 547, 40) the death of Shemseddīn Fenārī, without the verse, but with the phrase *decus illud Doctorum Europaeae Rumiliae* = مفخر العلماء الروم [sic], found only in Mz.

On the other hand, there are among these passages a few cases where Han. stood with other manuscripts against Mz:

8. Han. had (*H.M.* 530, 28), with *Ank*, the corruption: *cuiusdam e finitimis sanzacbegi.*
13. Han. had (*H.M.* 335, 9) the words omitted in Mz: . . . *filius Casis Burchanedinis ad Nasradinem Begum, Dulgadiris filium secessit. Nam . . .*
14. Han. had (*H.M.* 485, 38) the words omitted in Mz: *Secundum haec mandavit Mustapha suis, ut omnes ad Calliopolim naves reficerentur. Praefectos etiam . . . ad se deduci . . .*[1]

Furthermore:

(*a*) At *Mz* 21, 17 appears a second genealogy for Ertoghrul (taken by Neshrī from his second source),[2] on which Neshrī comments that this Ertoghrul must be different from 'Osmān's father. It is lacking at *Mn* 26, 7 and *Ank* 64, 14, and also at *H.M.* 100, 48.

(*b*) In Mz a short account of the disgrace of Ḥājji 'Ivaż is appended (*Mz* 155, 4–8) to the chapter on Murād II's

[1] As for (1), *H.M.* 338, 18 has, with Mz: *Bexenen*, but this is not significant, for it has also *Derendam*, lacking in both 'Āpz and Neshrī but found in *Anon.* 34, 22, and hence (presumably) standing in Ver.: Leunclavius is here harmonizing Han. and Ver.; (4) comes at a point where Han. no longer reflects Neshrī; (15) seems to be mistranslated (cf. *H.M.* 475, 48).

[2] It is lost from O.A. but is reproduced by Rūḥī, see *Mitt. z. Osm. Gesch.* ii. 135.

marriage to the Isfendiyār princess (= *'Āpz* § 94), while in *Mn* (228, 15), *Ank* (576, 11) and in Han. (*H.M.* 528, 40) it appears two chapters earlier.

(*c*) *Mz* 165, 2 (here following *'Āpz* 108, 22) lacks an addition found at *Mn* 242, 6, *Ank* 616, 13, and also in Han. (*H.M.* 547, 50): *una cum Isa bego Caramanoglio, Suleimane bego Dulgadiroglio, Zeinale Aladine, Casis Burchanedinis filio.*

(*d*) *Mz* 172, 15 adds to *'Āpz* 120, 25 the names of two more viziers, Shihābeddīn and Saruja (they appear at O.A. fol. 115v), who were to act as counsellors to the young Meḥemmed II; these two names are lacking at *Mn* 251, 13, *Ank* 646, 15, and also in Han. (*H.M.* 560, 6).

Thus the text lying behind Han. was not identical with Mz. It was, however, very close to it, usually agreeing with it against the consensus of the other manuscripts, and parting company with it only to ally itself with other manuscripts of Neshrī.

What do these divergences amount to? In the seven cases just noticed where Han. parts company with Mz, only one (8) represents an obvious deterioration of the text: (13) and (14) are proved, from 'Āpz, to be better readings; and (*a*) and (*b*), the dropping of one of two contradictory genealogies and the moving, apparently for stylistic reasons,[1] of a short anecdote added by Neshrī himself to his written sources, suggest not deterioration of the text but an author's revision of it.

In this light, (*c*) becomes very significant. Neshrī's source for this chapter, the account of Murād II's campaign against Karaman in 839, is *'Āpz* § 107, to which is appended, in all manuscripts and in Han., a note taken from the chronological list which records other, unrelated, events of that year. The further addition found in Han. and in all manuscripts except Mz, the catalogue of Murād's allies in the Karaman campaign (of whom 'Āpz makes no mention), represents a further borrowing from the list, whose wording

[1] The story is not given by 'Āpz or in O.A., but Neshrī would be interested in Ḥājji 'Ivaż, the hero of the defence of Bursa in 816/1413 (see p. 19, above). There is a brief mention of the '*vāḳi'a* of Ḥājji 'Ivaż' in the chronological lists, sub anno [828], and this no doubt prompted Neshrī to place the story where it appears in Mz, immediately after another 'event' of 828. Its position in *Mn/Ank/* Han. is also justifiable, however, for it there rounds off a chapter which began with Murād II's dispositions of the viziers so that 'only Ibrāhīm and Ḥājji 'Ivaż Pasha were left' (*Ank* 574, 13).

the Turkish manuscripts reproduce exactly.[1] The absence of the words in Mz represents therefore not a loss, but the state of the text before a reviser—who but Neshrī?—referred again to the source and took from it some extra lines to expand ʿĀpz's account. Similarly (*d*), the dropping from the text behind Han. of two names added in Mz, might represent a reviser's second thoughts.[2] Again, although the text lying behind Han. preserved Mz's order for the chapters of the 'first block' (p. 36, above), it does seem to have had the chapters of the 'second block' in the revised order which Mz's Arabic note enjoins (see p. 26) and which the author, in his first transcription of the draft text represented by Mz, would follow.[3]

Thus the text behind Han. was an improved, slightly revised version of Neshrī's History, lying between the early recension represented by Mz and the later recension of the other manuscripts, but much closer to the former than to the latter. This is precisely the description we should apply to the fair-copy version of the *Jihān-numā*: from this, and not from the independent 'History of the Oghuzian Turks', Han. seems to depend, so that the sequence proposed at p. 30 can be expanded thus:

(1) Draft for section six of the *Jihān-numā* = Codex Menzel

↓

(2) Fair copy version of section six of the *Jihān-numā*

↓ ↘ Codex Hanivaldanus

(3) 'History of the Oghuzian Turks'

This is tentative. But the identification of Wittek's X is beyond

[1] See Appendix III, entries for [839].

[2] Mz's lack of some words in (13) and (14) certainly arises from accident, but this, we now see, does not absolutely exclude the possibility that Mz is an autograph (pp. 27–29, above): in transcribing his draft Neshrī might have noticed his errors and corrected them, in his transcript, from ʿĀpz. Further indications that Neshrī referred back to his sources are given in Ch. VI.

[3] The Latin text suggests that the slip *üzerimize* (p. 22, above) had already—as we should expect—been corrected: 'Irruebant vero Turcorum in aciem nubis instar nigrae' (*H.M.* 553, 2).

doubt; his schema (p. 10), with the possible intervening link ignored, now reads:

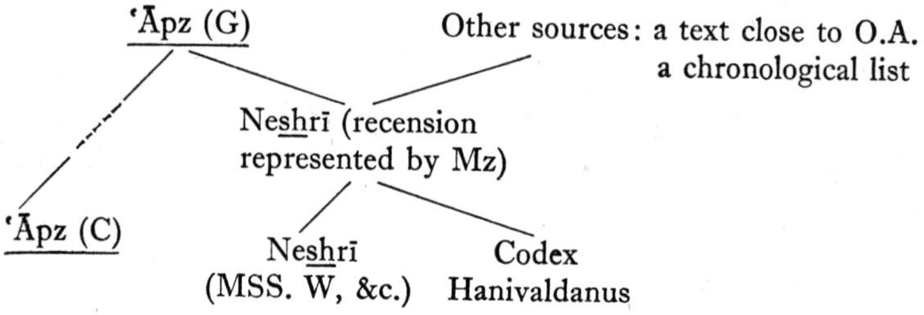

VI

THE LATER RECENSION

THE critical apparatus of *Ank* does not inspire such confidence in its accuracy as to encourage one to draw deductions from the detailed variants which it records; all the same, with the help of Mz it is possible to construct, on the criterion of their scope and content, the following stemma[1] for the manuscripts on which *Ank* is based:

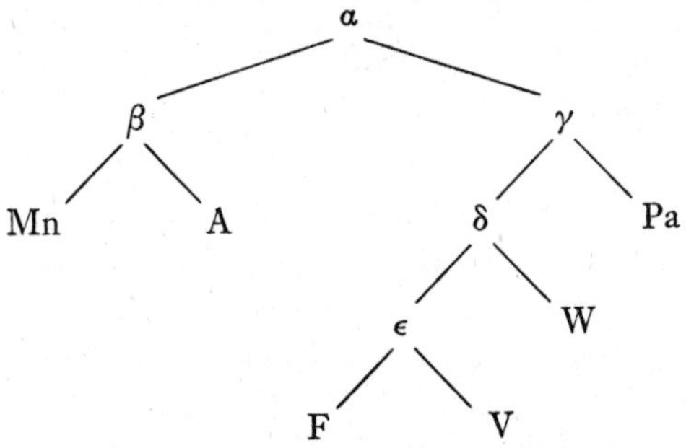

Taeschner, pointing to the presence in this later and revised recension (α, as attested by the consensus of all the manuscripts except Mz) of so many manifest corruptions, was inclined to believe that the reviser cannot have been Neshrī himself.[2] But this is not necessarily conclusive, for the corruptions could have crept in between Neshrī's autograph of the revised text and the archetype (α) of the surviving manuscripts. Are there in the revised recension any positive indications—additions or alterations—to suggest that the reviser was in fact Neshrī?

The passage cited by Taeschner as being demonstrably an interpolation into the text of Mz (*Ank* 134, 14–19, lacking at *Mz*

[1] The arguments for the construction of this stemma are given in Appendix IV, p. 81. The latest and most complete list of the known manuscripts is given by Taeschner, in his introductions to *Mz* and *Mn*, with references to the catalogues and to the earlier lists by Fahriye Arık and F. R. Unat (*Bakış*, 182 ff.). I reproduce here only the essential details, with some observations resulting from my own inspection of Mn and a few Istanbul manuscripts in 1958–9.

[2] *Mn* (*Einl.*), 11–13.

39, 21)[1] describes the founding by associates of Orkhān of the first mosque to be built in the newly-conquered Bursa. It is also absent at *H.M.* 173, 21: 'Ceterum anno superius indicato captam fuisse Burusam hauddubie constat: sed an superstes fuerit Osman . . . ambigitur'; thus this interpolation (and, so far as one can judge, the other additions and alterations next to be considered) was made later than those dealt with at pp. 37–39, above, which, appearing already in Han., I believe to have been introduced into the fair copy of the *Jihān-numā*.

This is not the only case where an addition common to all manuscripts of the revised recension reveals a familiarity with Bursa and its history. We have noticed above (p. 35, passages (*b*) and (*c*)) an account, with many details of local topography, of Orkhān's buildings at Bursa and a story of the Karaman-oghlu's stratagem when besieging the town. To these may be added:

1. *Mn* 41, 10/*Ank* 104, 11 (lacking at *Mz* 31, 21 and *H.M.* 138, 49): '(*Brusa ḥiṣārında* +) *Manastırda*'.
2. *Mn* 78, 10–12/*Ank* 184, 16–18 (lacking at *Mz* 51, 16 and *H.M.* 211, 55): Suleymān Pasha's foundation of a mosque at Bursa and his virtues.
3. *Mn* 82, 3–4/*Ank* 196, 8–10 (lacking at *Mz* 53, 21 and *H.M.* 227, 40): Kara Rustem's *türbe* at Bursa.
4. *Mn* 149, 3–9/*Ank* 356, 10–16[2] (lacking at *Mz* 97, 4 and *H.M.* 350, 49): the pillaging of Bursa by Timur's son.

Given the tradition that Neshrī lived at Bursa, these insertions, not to be found (so far as I can see) in any of his sources, could well be by Neshrī himself, writing from his local knowledge. Yet this is not conclusive: they might be the work of an anonymous redactor who knew the town.

Some other alterations to the text are more decisive:

1. At *Mz* 18, 15–19, the concluding lines of his *ṭabaḳa* on the Seljuks where Neshrī is endeavouring to fit the legendary material on the rise of the Ottomans into the context of the political history of Anatolia, he carefully distinguishes two sultans ʿAlāeddīn of Konya, emphasizing that ʿOsmān was the contemporary of the

[1] *Mn* (*Einl.*), 7, and cf. p. 20, above.

[2] The apparatus for *Ank* 356, misplaced to the last five lines of 355, shows that the further addition *Ank* 356, 7–10 appears only in MS. A, on which see pp. 47–49, below.

second and not, as was erroneously believed, of the first. In *Mn* 22, 3–10/*Ank* 52, 9–19 this passage is expanded to clarify further the distinction, which at a later point too (*Mn* 27, 5–7/*Ank* 68, 5–6, lacking at *Mz* 22, 18) is emphasized again.[1]

2. Neshrī knows various traditions for the capture of Gelibolu. At *Mz* 51, 9 (= *Ank* 184, 3) he reproduces the statement of 'Āpz (47, 5) that it was surrendered to Suleymān Pasha, but adds his own note that 'trustworthy authorities'[2] maintain that Suleymān died before Gelibolu was taken; hence at *Mz* 52, 18 (= *Ank* 192, 7), where too he is following 'Āpz (48, 7), he alters 'Āpz's 'Murād [I] passed through Gelibolu' (which for 'Āpz is already in Ottoman hands) to 'Murād took Gelibolu'. At *Mn* 80, 12–13/*Ank* 192, 10–11 the reviser has added a further note[3] to emphasize that Murād, and not Suleymān Pasha, took the town.

3. At *Mz* 83, 5 the first of the two long interpolations from the text related to O.A. ends with the account of the assassination of Murād I at Kosova: he was, says Neshrī following this source, killed with a dagger by an unnamed, wounded assailant; Neshrī then returns to 'Āpz (58, 4) for the account of the precautions taken immediately afterwards. At *Mn* 129, 15–18/*Ank* 304, 6–9[4] there is inserted, shortly before this transition, a passage in which the assailant, now named as 'Milosh Kupili', seeks out Murād unwounded, but receives a wound on the way. *The reviser has referred again to the text of 'Āpz*: finding there (57, 25) the tradition according to which Murād was killed by Milosh Kupili, who was *not* wounded (and used a lance), he has blended the two accounts together by adding to the version of Mz the name of the assailant and causing him to be wounded before he encountered Murād.

4. At *Mz* 98 Neshrī, using his two main sources, is describing events immediately after the battle of Ankara. Following 'Āpz (72, 17) he writes (line 8): 'Meḥemmed returned to Amasya.'

[1] The chapter containing the earlier passage is not reproduced in *H.M.* at all (it and all the preceding chapters may not have figured in Han.). The expansion at the later point seems not to have stood in Han. (cf. *H.M.* 102, 16): but here Leunclavius is making his own harmony with what he has recorded before, mainly from Byzantine authors.

[2] Perhaps his chronological list, which must have ascribed the capture of Gelibolu to Murād I (see Appendix III, sub anno [755]): comparison with the earlier lists published by Atsız and Turan shows that in the later ones these first items have become disarranged.

[3] It is lacking at *H.M.* 220, 4.

[4] But not at *H.M.* 301, 37.

'Āpz then continues: ''Īsā and Mūsā fought in the Bursa district; Mūsā drove out 'Īsā and ruled at Bursa'; but Neshrī has turned to his other source, which, on the evidence of O.A. (fol. 46ʳ), gave him his next words: ''Īsā occupied Bursa . . ., Mūsā had been taken prisoner with his father'. Neshrī proceeds: 'Their story will be told in detail'—as it is, in the second long interpolation from the second source; but for a few more lines he reverts to *'Āpz* 72, 18, just beyond the point from which he had digressed, and reproduces from it (line 10): 'Emīr Suleymān came to Bursa; Mūsā fled and went to Karaman.' In *Mn* 151, 7/*Ank* 364, 11, however, this last 'Mūsā' has been changed to ''Isā'.[1] This is no accident: the reviser has realized that according to what precedes Mūsā is a prisoner, and it must be 'Īsā who was driven out by Suleymān.

5. At *Mz* 172, 8–10 Neshrī's chapter on the battle of the Zlatitsa Pass, mainly based on the first half of *'Āpz* § 117, concludes with a sentence taken from his other source: where 'Āpz (120, 17–18) says merely that 'Khalīl Pasha's brother' was ransomed, the second source (cf. O.A. fol. 115ʳ) gives Neshrī both the name of the brother, Maḥmūd Čelebi, and the detail that his wife, Murād II's sister, interceded with the Sultan to procure his ransom. In *Mn* 251, 8/*Ank* 646, 8[2] there is added the further detail, *also found at this point in O.A.* (but absent in 'Āpz), that the price of the ransom was the surrender of Semendre. The reviser has referred again to the source which Neshrī used.

Thus in (1) and (2) the reviser is at pains to emphasize details which Neshrī (as represented in Mz) had felt to be important; (3) and (5) show the reviser going back to each of Neshrī's main sources for detail which Neshrī had overlooked in the recension of Mz and Han.; and (4) shows him smoothing out an inconsistency which had escaped Neshrī's attention as he harmonized his two sources. It was at this stage of revision too that the Koran story was transferred to 'Osmān, and the chapters of the 'first block' (p. 26, above) were rearranged in consequence. These modifications, which show the reviser to be influenced by the same concern for narrative and chronological consistency which Neshrī

[1] These lines (*Mz* 98, 10–14/*Ank* 364, 11–19) are omitted in *H.M.* (after 371, 42), Leunclavius substituting his own comments on the savage strife 'novorum Cadmeorum fratrum, Baiasitis filiorum'.

[2] But not at *H.M.* 559, 37.

exhibits, bear the stamp of a *historian*'s revising hand. There is no reason to doubt that this historian was Neshrī himself.

It may be objected that this hypothesis of a further stage of revision by the author, after the draft had been transcribed in fair copy, is over-complicated. But not only are there indications enough from other texts that Ottoman historians produced more than one 'edition' of their works;[1] the textual evidence for this work tallies perfectly with Neshrī's own testimony that section six of the *Jihān-numā* was 'separated off' to stand as an independent work. The occasion of these further revisions was, I suggest, this 'separation', at which time, presumably, the stylistic revision too was made.

THE HYPARCHETYPE β

The hyparchetype β was in content very close to α, for the manuscripts depending from it, Mn and A, seem to share no additions not already attested for α; the principal change which it made was to substitute Persian chapter-headings for Turkish.

MS. Mn (= *Manisa, Muradiye* 1373/1)

[Mn, undated, was used for *Ank* (siglum M) and published in facsimile by Taeschner (*Mn*). It is described by Taeschner, *Mz* (*Einl.*), 16–17, and *Mn* (*Einl.*), 13–17. Two long gaps are supplied in *Mn* (42–64, 89–111) from Pa.]

Taeschner is fully justified in regarding Mn as the most conservative representative of the revised recension.[2] His judgement on its age, however, requires modification.

On the evidence of its hand, Taeschner followed the Turkish editors (*Ank* xii) in ascribing Mn to the fifteenth century. Mn is certainly very old: on a visit to Manisa in 1959 I saw the manuscript and copied this prominent watermark, appearing in the

[1] e.g. 'Āshiḳpashazāde's History, for which P. Wittek postulated five recensions (*Orientalische Literaturzeitung*, 34, 1931, 698–707); Shukrullāh's *Bahjat al-tawārīkh*, one manuscript of which, the presentation copy to Maḥmūd Pasha, differs slightly in content from the others (see Ç. N. Atsız, *Osmanlı tarihleri*, i, 1949, 41); and Idrīs's *Hasht Bihisht*: the date 919/1513–4 in the colophon of the heavily corrected autograph Esad Ef. 2197 (see M. Šükrü, in *Der Islam*, xix, 1931, 133) shows that the version presented to Selīm I differed from that written for Bāyezīd II.

[2] *Mn* (*Einl.*), 13–17.

margins of fols. 4–5, which proves to be a somewhat deteriorated version of a mark (Briquet, no. 15891) found in the paper of Venetian documents written in the last quarter of the fifteenth century. This indeed strongly supports the ascription of the manuscript to a date before 1500.

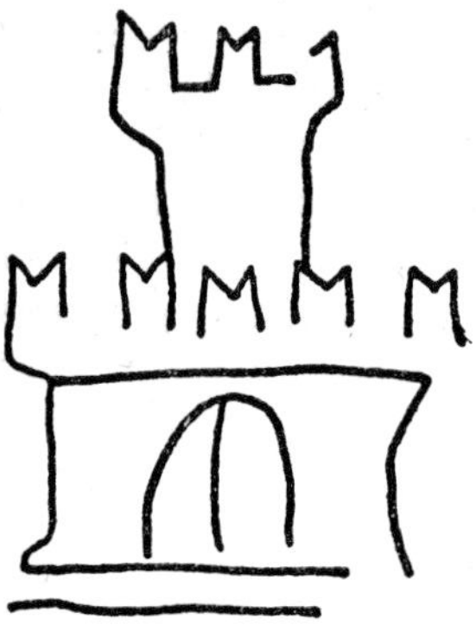

Internal evidence for the date of copying is to be gleaned, however, from the 'summary-chapters' on the viziers and the 'ulemā, for here a copyist (as well as an author modernizing his source, see p. 9) may modify the biographical details given by the author in order to bring the account up to date. In Mn's chapter on the viziers we find two significant modifications, indications that by the time of copying both Ibrāhīm Pasha (Čandarlı) and Fā'iḳ Pasha were dead;[1] so that Mn cannot have been written before 905 (beginning 8 August 1499). Mn's chapter on the 'ulemā allows us to bring this terminus forward. Among many modifications to the text of Mz, Mn names, as additions to Mz's list of the holy men who flourished under Meḥemmed II, three 'ulemā and three sheykhs;[2] and whereas in Mz this section ends (233, 7) with a present tense: *bunlar dakhi ṣāḥib-kerāmet kishilerdür*, Mn (325, 17) has a past tense: *kishiler-idi*. Mn makes no additions to Mz's list of holy men for the reign of Bāyezīd II, merely reproducing the names of Sheykh Muḥyīeddīn Iskilibī and Sheykh Ilāhī; it adds, however, immediately afterwards, the *du'ā* رحمة الله عليهم اجمعين, showing that for the copyist of Mn they are all dead. The last of them to die was Muḥyīeddīn Iskilibī (whose name appears at only one remove from the final *du'ā*); he lived into the reign of Selīm I, who appointed him to the

[1] *Mz* 229, 15: '*Ibrāhīm Pasha . . . ghāyet ṣāḥib-i khayr kishidür*', but *Mn* 321, 10: '. . . *-idi*'; *Mz* 231, 5: '*Fā'iḳ Pasha: dakhi niyyetdedür*', but *Mn* 323, 5: '. . . *-idi*'. According to Sa'deddīn (ii. 95–96 and 217), Ibrāhīm Pasha died in the first days of 905: the precise date 20 Dhu 'l-Ḥijja [904] (= 29 July 1499), which may well be better, is given in the 'Neshrī' MS. Pb, fol. 82r (see the passage quoted at p. 83, below); here also Fā'iḳ Pasha is said to have died in 905.

[2] Most of these changes seem to be peculiar to Mn (or to the hyparchetype β), for of Mn's six extra names (the Mollas Luṭfī, Akhawayn, and Yigen-oghlu 'Alī, and the Sheykhs Bolılı, Ṣūfiyeddīn, and Ḥabībī 'Omarī, *Mn* 325, lines 12, 15, 16) only the last appears in W (see F. Giese, *Textrez.* 50).

prominent office of ḳāḍī'asker of Rumili, and died in 920/1514.[1] Mn cannot therefore have been copied earlier than the reign of Selīm I.

This conclusion is supported by the fact that Mn's text ends with this *du'ā*, thus omitting not only the final chapter, the recapitulation of the pious works of Bāyezīd II, but also the *ḳaṣīde* in his praise which closes the work.[2] This casual ending suggests that, the Sultan being dead, Mn's copyist was less concerned to show him the honour that Neshrī had done him.

The full vocalization of Mn and its provenance suggest that it may have been written as a textbook for an Ottoman prince.[3]

MS. A (= *Istanbul, Asariatika müzesi*, 479)

[A was used for *Ank* and is described by Taeschner, *Mz* (*Einl.*), 18–19. It was completed in 969/1561 by a certain 'Alī b. 'Abdullāh. A few pages are lost at the beginning (text begins at *Ank* 36, 1).]

A, the other manuscript depending from the hyparchetype β, contains more numerous and more extensive additions to the basic text than any other manuscript. The sources for some of these can be identified:

(1) Aḥmedī's *Iskender-nāme* was recognized by the editors of *Ank* to be the source of most of A's interpolated verse-passages (*Ank* 56, 66, 78, &c., the last—much out of place—being at 660).

(2) One recension of Uruj's *History of the Ottoman House* has supplied several short prose insertions, e.g.:

i. *Ank* 70, 5 (apparatus): ''Osmān was born in Rūm; Ertoghrul set him to the plough as a youth', cf. Uruj (ed. F. Babinger), 6, 18–21.

ii. *Ank* 106, 6 (app.): ''Alāeddīn presented 'Osmān with the sword of the Caliph 'Osmān', cf. Uruj, 10, 16–18.

iii. *Ank* 120, 2–3 (app.): Köse Mikhal's dream of the Prophet, cf. Uruj, 9, 20 ff.

iv. *Ank* 154, 5–6 (text): Orkhān sends to Ḥājji Bektash for *ijāzet*, cf. Uruj, 16, 1.

v. *Ank* 168, 10 (app.); Baba Ilyās, cf. Uruj, 11, 2 ff.

[1] Tashköprüzāde (Rescher), 222 f. = (Mejdī), 349 ff., and hence Sa'deddīn, ii. 576–7.

[2] The *ḳaṣīde* is found in MS. A, and thus had figured in β.

[3] See p. 9 and p. 34, n. 2, above.

vi. *Ank* 354, 18–356, 4:[1] the story of the Iron Cage, cf. Uruj, 35, 18 ff.

vii. *Ank* 360, 17–362, 4: the suicide of Bāyezīd I, cf. Uruj, 37, 8 ff.

(3) Shukrullāh's *Bahjat al-tawārīkh*, probably not in the original Persian but in a Turkish translation of the chapter on the Ottomans,[2] has supplied:

i. *Ank* 308, 5 (app.): Murād I's *türbe*, cf. Shukrullāh (ed. T. Seif), 92, 12.

ii. *Ank* 516, 10–12: the virtues of Meḥemmed I, cf. Shukrullāh, 106, 7 ff.

iii. *Ank* 530, 16 (app.): Meḥemmed I's Karaman campaign, cf. Shukrullāh, 108, 1 ff.

iv. *Ank* 536, 3–4 (app.): victories of Meḥemmed I, cf. Shukrullāh, 110, 11 ff.

v. *Ank* 546, 18–548, 7: the pious works of Meḥemmed I, cf. Shukrullāh, 108, 5 ff.

vi. *Ank* 676, 7–14 and 676, 16–678, 11: the pious works of Murād II, cf. Shukrullāh, 114, 15–116, 5 and 112, 18–114, 12.

A contains also several short excursus, without real factual detail, on the organization of newly-conquered territories (e.g. *Ank* 314, 8 (app.); 586, 17–19; 754, 2–4) and conventional bombastic descriptions of battles (*Ank* 576, 1 (app.); 610, 12–15 (app.); 774, 17 (app.); 782, 2–3 (app.)); for these, perhaps, and for a few scattered verses (*Ank* 228, 3–4; 458, 14), we need not seek a written source. Elsewhere, however, we find further extensive interpolations which do contain factual detail. A few are written in simple, popular style—an account of how Meḥemmed I tried to rescue Bāyezīd from Timur, encamped near Sivriḥiṣār (*Ank* 368, 3–13), extra details on Emīr Suleymān's siege of Sivriḥiṣār (*Ank* 470, 1–10 and 478, 16–19), and a long story of the Karaman-oghlu's siege of the same town and a miracle of the local saint ʿAlī Dede

[1] The apparatus is displaced here, see p. 356, last line.

[2] The British Museum MS. Or. 11155 (23 ff. with 15 lines to the page, undated) is a Turkish translation, made in the reign of Bāyezīd II, of the Ottoman chapter of the *Bahjat al-tawārīkh*, to which the anonymous translator has appended a summary account of the events of the reign of Meḥemmed II and of the first years of Bāyezīd II (to the Kili-Akkerman campaign of 889/1484). There are in MS. A's insertions striking echoes of the wording of this translation.

(*Ank* 636, 10–642, 4); these seem to be based on tales and traditions current at Sivriḥiṣār, which was perhaps the home of the redactor.

Most of the long interpolations, however, are written in a very elevated style, adorned with Turkish verses: they concern particularly the second battle of Kosova (*Ank* 660, 15–662, 18; 664, 7–672, 5), the siege of Constantinople (*Ank* 688, 19–704, 13) and the defeat of Uzun Ḥasan (*Ank* 800, 9 (app.); 800, 18–802, 5; 804, 19–806, 7; 806, 9–19; 816, 6 (app.)). These would appear to be taken from a literary source, perhaps early; but I am unable to identify it.[1]

There are no grounds whatever for imagining that any of these additions were made by Neshrī himself, and it is the main blemish of *Ank* that its editors, apparently assuming that they were (*Ank* xv), have promoted many of them—but not all—to their text. A in fact deserves to rank as a new compilation, and its compiler—presumably the ʿAlī b. ʿAbdullāh who completed the manuscript in 969/1561—to be counted as an 'historian' in his own right.

THE HYPARCHETYPE γ

The hyparchetype γ was, in content, further removed from α than was β, for it had received several interpolations: the apparatus of *Ank* records, in the nearly completed published text, some fifteen. A number of these are little more than glosses.[2] The major interpolations are:[3]

[1] A has an interesting addition at *Ank* 296, 9–298, 5 (in the course of Neshrī's first long interpolation from the source related to O.A.), which describes an artillery engagement at the first battle of Kosova. The style is indistinguishable from what precedes and follows: either the redactor of A has expanded the narrative with a clever pastiche of the style of the source, or he has consulted the source and written in a passage which Neshrī chose to omit. There is in fact good reason why Neshrī should have omitted a passage describing the use of cannon, for it conflicts with ʿĀpz's statement (60, 20, reproduced by Neshrī at *Mz* 89, 2/*Ank* 326, 1) that at the time of Bāyezīd I's siege of Constantinople a few years later cannon were not common. It seems possible that the redactor of A, with Neshrī's source before him, has 'corrected' Neshrī's deliberate omission (cf. also A's variant 'cannon-fire' for 'arrows' at *Ank* 298, 9; the redactor may also have gone back to the source for the verses at *Ank* 228, 4 and 276, 10–11, and for the prose additions 276, 12–15 and 294, 13–19).

[2] e.g. *Ank* 144, 15–16 (why the dome was called '*gümüshlü*'), 154, 19–155, 1 (on the *yamak*s), 300, 7–11 (on the criers called (?) *boz-ünji*, cf. 650, 14), 710, 11 (*Zeytunlık*, the old name of the Palace site), 756, 2–3 (Ḥamza Beg was sanjak-bey of Nigebolu), 822, 3–4 (Ḳāsim Pasha's chronogram for the battle of Terjan).

[3] Some of these have been noticed above (pp. 35–36) in the discussion of the

1. *Ank* 116, 8–14: a skirmish during the siege of Bursa by ʿOsmān Ghāzī.
2. *Ank* 530, 7–534, 4: additions to the account of Meḥemmed I's Karaman campaign (the Sultan's illness and treatment by the poet and physician Sheykhī, Bāyezīd Pasha's deception of the Karaman-oghlu). The story is continued with later interpolations: the Karaman-oghlu's breaking of his oath (534, 10–19), and his death, seen as retribution for this perjury (590, 17–19).
3. *Ank* 572, 16–574, 8: a story of Mezīd Beg, who had supervised the execution of 'Küčük' Muṣṭafā.
4. *Ank* 592, 13–19 and 596, 9–598, 3: stories of Yorguč Pasha.
5. *Ank* 606, 1–7: the extravagance of the Germiyan-oghlu Yaʿḳūb.
6. *Ank* 650, 2–652, 6: incidents during the battle of Varna.
7. *Ank* 652, 18–654, 6: the sending of the head of the Hungarian king to Bursa.

One small omission in γ may be significant: at *Ank* 812, 14 for the '*Dā'ūd Pasha-i kāmrān, Āṣaf-i zamān*' of Mz (210, 18) and β it had simply '*Dā'ūd Pasha*', perhaps an indication that the redaction of γ was made after Dā'ūd Pasha's dismissal from the Grand Vizierate in 902/1497.[1] Yet it cannot have been made long after, for the Neshrī MS. used by Idrīs Bidlīsī (writing between 908 and 911) stemmed from this hyparchetype, as is revealed by the appearance in his *Hasht Bihisht* of some of the interpolations characteristic of this recension.[2] There are hints also in the text

discrepancies between Han. and MS. W, but of the seven passages listed there none seems to be peculiar to W: (*b*) and (*c*) are common to all manuscripts of the revised recension (and hence stood in α); (*a*), (*e*), (*f*), (*g*), common to the manuscripts depending from γ, reappear here as (1), (3), (6), (7); for (*d*) the apparatus of *Ank* is silent, but as it is lacking at *Mn* 226, 18 it too is probably a γ-passage. Needless to say, (2), (4), and (5), as well as the others, are absent in *H.M.* (cf. 472, 51, 473, 23, 535, 50; 536, 44, 538, 25; 542, 11).

[1] Dā'ūd Pasha was Grand Vizier from 888/1483 to 902/1497 (*EI*², s.v., by M. Tayyib Gökbilgin), i.e. throughout the period when Neshrī was working.

[2] Idrīs reproduces (without, admittedly, naming his source) the substance of passages (2), (4), and (5) (British Museum MS. Add. 7646, fols. 225ʳ–226ᵛ, 257ᵛ, 259ᵛ = Katība V, Dastān 24, Katība VI, Dastāns 5 and 6, respectively). That these had stood in Idrīs's 'first edition', commissioned by Bāyezīd in 908, is proved by the presence of the first two in Bihishtī's History (British Museum MS. Add. 7869, fols. 110ᵛ, 108ᵛ), completed in 917, which depends on it (see *EI*², s.v. Bihishtī).

If the recension of γ was in existence by 908 (beg. 7 July 1502), the revised

of Kemālpashazāde[1] and clear signs in that of Saʿdeddīn[2] that this was the recension of Neshrī's History which they used.

MS. Pa (= *Paris, Bibl. Nat. supp. turc* 153)

[Pa was used for *Ank* and is described by Taeschner, *Mz* (*Einl.*), 19–20. Facsimiles of its relevant pages fill the lacunae in *Mn*. Copied before 1050/1640, it lacks only the final *ḳaṣīde*.]

This fairly old manuscript, nearly complete, is, as Taeschner's sample analysis of its variants (*Mn* (*Einl.*), 14–15) shows and the stemma confirms, the best of those depending from the hyparchetype γ; though in content further removed from α than Mn, the only conservative representative of the β-group, in verbal detail it is closer to Mz (and hence to α) than Mn.[3] It appears to contain no additions of its own in the text, but an owner of the manuscript has added several parallel passages in the margin. Most of these he has taken from a manuscript in the Type W_1 recension of the *Anonymous Chronicles* (i.e. the text as published by F. Giese);[4] two follow Solakzāde almost verbatim.[5]

MS. W (= *Vienna, H.O.* 15)

[On W is based the text of *Ank* (siglum Vy). It is described by Taeschner, *Mz* (*Einl.*), 17. Completed in 966/1558, it lacks only one leaf (= *Ank* 2, 17–6, 13).]

This manuscript, old, nearly complete, and easily accessible to German scholars, has, ever since it was used by Hammer, been

recension was, *a fortiori*, made earlier, i.e. almost certainly within Neshrī's lifetime: this seems to me to remove any doubt whether Neshrī himself was the reviser.

[1] Kemālpashazāde (book vii, facsimile, ed. Ş. Turan, Ankara, 1954) has, for example, at points where he is certainly following Neshrī, the 'glosses' (p. 49, n. 2, above) *Zeytunlık* (p. 102), 'sanjak-bey of Nigebolu' (p. 212), and the chronogram (p. 405).

[2] Saʿdeddīn reproduces the substance of passages (2), (4), and (7) at i. 278 ff., i. 332 and 335–6, and i. 383 respectively, in two cases explicitly on the authority of Neshrī (cf. p. 278, line 11; p. 383, line 12).

[3] Taeschner's sample shows that in 38 cases where Mz shares variants with (and hence authenticates the readings of) manuscripts of the revised recension, Pa agrees in 30 cases with Mz, against Mn's 17 (and W's 14).

[4] e.g. apparatus to *Ank* 58, 13 and 19; to *Ank* 336, 8; to *Ank* 336, 16–17; to *Ank* 590, 15; cf. *Anon.* 4, 19–22, 5, 4–6; 30, 21–31, 19; 33, 7–11; 60, 20–63, 1 respectively.

[5] Apparatus to *Ank* 200, 18 and 714, 13–14, cf. Solakzāde (Istanbul, 1298), 32 and 214 respectively.

the foundation for nearly all studies on Neshrī's History; this spurious authority induced the editors of *Ank* to choose it as the basis of their text, although the better manuscripts Mn and Pa were available to them. It seems to contain no additions of its own.

MS. V (= *Istanbul, Veliyeddin* 2351)

[Used for *Ank* (though its variants are noted only for 2–146, 686–842) and described by Taeschner, *Mz* (*Einl.*), 20–21. It was copied, in 1066/1656, from a defective exemplar which lacked the first leaf (text begins at *Ank* 4, 2), and lacks also the final chapter and the *ḳaṣīde*.]

V contains a long interpolation (from fol. 195^r) relating the 'Legendary History of Constantinople', which (on inspecting the manuscript in 1959) I found to be the version of the W_3 recension of the *Anonymous Chronicles*. The summary chapters with which Neshrī rounded off his work are in V succeeded (fol. 268^v) by a short chapter on the ages of the sultans and the lengths of their reigns, and a continuation to the year 955 (fols. 269^r–335^v): the latter also is based on the W_3 recension of the *Anonymous Chronicles* (it begins with the words of *Anon.* 117, 22 ff. and ends with those of *Anon.* 150, 19) but contains numerous and extensive additions. The compiler has added in the body of the Neshrī text also several dates (also from *Anon.*),[1] and a few topographical glosses.[2]

MS. F (= *Istanbul, Fatih-Millet, Ali Emiri tarih* 220)

[Used for *Ank*, described by Taeschner, *Mz* (*Einl.*), 20. F contains only the third ('Ottoman') *ṭabaḳa*; it lacks the *ḳaṣīde*.]

F, apparently not very old, has received no additions beyond those common to the manuscripts depending from γ.

Five further manuscripts are known. E, = Esad Efendi (Istanbul, Süleymaniye) 2080, was known to, but not used by, the editors of *Ank*. It is described by Taeschner, *Mz* (*Einl.*), 22. Slightly defective at the beginning and end, it belongs to the revised

[1] e.g. *Ank* 730, 3; 746, 8 and 748, 9; 770, 12; cf. *Anon.* 111, 28; 112, 7; 112, 25 respectively.

[2] e.g. *Ank* 686, 17–19; 688, 4; 690, 15–16.

recension.[1] S, = Saray (Istanbul, Hazine 1361), dated 1131/1719, purports to be complete but in fact contains little more than the first half of the text.[2] The other three are copies of extant manuscripts N[öldeke] of W, T[ürk Tarih Kurumu] of V, and Y[ınanç] of T.[3]

Two manuscripts, 'B' and 'Ab', which Taeschner lists on the authority of Unat, do not in fact contain Neshrī's History.[4] Pb and D are considered in Ch. VII.

[1] E was copied from a defective exemplar, as its text begins on fol. 1^{v} with the words of *Ank* 28, 2. It breaks off short at *Mz* 232, 17, having lost one or two leaves at the end. It contains (I found) at fol. 26^{r} the interpolation on the founding of a mosque at Bursa (pp. 41–42, above), and thus must belong to the revised recension.

[2] S is described by Taeschner, *Mz* (*Einl.*), 22, and now by F. E. Karatay, *Topkapı Sarayı Müzesi Kütüphanesi: türkçe yazmalar kataloğu*, Istanbul, 1961, i, 208. On inspecting it I found that its text has by some accident (not misbinding) become disarranged, so that fols. 1^{v}–184^{r} = *Ank* 2, 3–266, 12; fols. 184^{r}–289^{r} = *Ank* 320, 17–466, 7; fols. 289^{r}–329^{v} = *Ank* 266, 14–320, 16. The text ends اول قشی بروسه‌ده قشلادی تم بعون الله تعالی وحسن توفیقه سنه ۱۱۳۱.

[3] *Mz* (*Einl.*), 17, 21.

[4] B = Bağdadlı Vehbi (Istanbul, Süleymaniye) 1233 is wrongly listed as a Neshrī in *İstanbul kütüphaneleri tarih-coğrafya yazmaları katalogları* i/2, 1944, 210, but had been correctly identified by L. Forrer (in *Der Islam*, xxvi, 1942, 178) as a manuscript of the *Anonymous Chronicles*. It begins as Type W_1, but is incomplete: the copyist has omitted (at fol. 88^{r}) the 'Legendary History' and abandoned his work at the bottom of fol. 90^{v} (= *Anon.* 113, 6), the last five leaves being blank.

Ab = Istanbul, Asariatika müzesi, 480, first described as a copy of the so-called 'History of Rustem Pasha' by Unat (*Bakış*, 185), was noted as such by Taeschner, *Mz* (*Einl.*), 23. In his communication to the Twenty-third (Cambridge, 1954) Congress of Orientalists, Unat claimed that it was a Neshrī, and was hence followed by Taeschner, *Mn* (*Einl.*), 17. On examining the manuscript in 1959 I found that it is certainly the 'History of Rustem Pasha': it begins as MS. Istanbul University Library T 2438 and ends as MS. Belediye, Cevdet O 106 (= L. Forrer's abridged translation, *Die osmanische Chronik des Rustem Pascha*, Leipzig, 1923, 178).

In a footnote in *T'OEM*, no. 11, p. 702, Khalīl Edhem referred to a manuscript in private hands entitled '*Tevārīkh-i Oghuziyān ilākh.*', whose author, he said, was Neshrī. The title indicates that it was probably a 'Rustem Pasha', for the Rustem Pasha MSS. 'Ab' (above), Cambridge 167, and Yozgat (see F. R. Unat, *Bakış*, 185) all bear the title *Tevārīkh-i Oghuziyān ve Jengiziyān ve Seljukiyān ve 'Osmāniyān.*

At *Mz* (*Einl.*), 23, Taeschner notes a report that the Istanbul MS. Revan 2058 is a Neshrī; according to the manuscript handlist of the collection, however, this is a manuscript of the *Kashf al-ẓunūn*.

VII

THE ABRIDGED RECENSION OF MSS. Pb AND D

MS. Pb (= Paris, Bibliothèque Nationale, supp. turc 1183) was used by the Turkish editors for their edition. In their introduction (*Ank* xi) they describe it as representing a text, dedicated to Selīm I, which Neshrī himself had made, abridging his work and providing it with a continuation down to the conquest of Egypt (in 923/1517); the passages which it has in common with other manuscripts read, they say, apart from slight variants, as the Vienna manuscript (W). In a communication to the Twenty-third (Cambridge, 1954) International Congress of Orientalists,[1] F. R. Unat spoke of a further and earlier (late-sixteenth-century?) manuscript—D[2]—donated in 1950 to the Dil ve Tarih-Coğrafya Fakültesi of Ankara University, which presented the same recension as Pb. Repeating his claim that this text represented a revision made by Neshrī for presentation to Selīm I, Unat announced that the continuation (whose text is to be published in the third volume of *Ank*) contained a number of autobiographical references.

Though they claim to have used Pb for their edition, the Turkish editors cease in fact to list its variants after *Ank* 240 (= *Mz* 66, MS. Pb, fol. 33^{v}). Examination of the manuscript[3] shows the reason: after its first thirty leaves or so (out of eighty-eight) Pb presents a text so severely and arbitrarily abridged that one page (containing 25 lines) of Pb represents anything up to ten pages (each containing 19 lines) of *Ank*, so that the listing of its variants within the confines of an apparatus is impossible. It is unlikely that such a mutilation of his work should have been made by Neshrī himself, and further examination of the text of Pb shows that his authorship of this recension is highly improbable.

[1] Later published as 'Müverrih Mehmet Neşri'nin eseri ve hayatı hakkında', *Belleten*, xxi, 1957, 297–300.

[2] My siglum: Taeschner, *Mn* (*Einl.*), 17, designates it S = Sarhan, the name of the donor, not noticing that he has already given this siglum to S[aray].

[3] By the courtesy of the authorities of the Bibliothèque Nationale I have a microfilm of Pb.

The year in which the redactor of the abridged text was working is revealed by his peculiar method of expressing dates. For the date A.H. 300, for example, he writes هجرتك سنه ٣٠٠ / ٦٢٠, with the note above الى غاية سنه ٩٢٠, 'to the terminus 920';[1] i.e., calculating from the year 920 (beginning 26 Feb. 1514) he writes below the Hijra date '300' the 'retrospective' date '620 [years ago]'. Though *Ank* records only a few examples in the apparatus,[2] the redactor uses this double dating consistently (if not always accurately) until almost the end of the text, the dates in the later part of the continuation running 915/5, 916/4, 917/3, and 919/1, but with a simple '920' five pages from the end. 920 is evidently the year in which he made his abridgement and wrote his continuation up to that point. His last pages, devoted to Selīm's campaigns against Persia and Egypt, carry the story further, so that at fol. 86^r appears 'Muḥarrem 921', at fol. 87^r 'Ṣafar 922', and at fol. 88^r his latest date 'Jumādā I [923]' (beginning 22 May 1517).

The continuation begins (fol. 79^r), after the 'summary-chapter' on the viziers,[3] with a chapter describing Hersek-zāde Aḥmed Pasha's defeat in Cilicia in 891/1486. The first indication that this continuation is not the work of Neshrī is its style: the continuator frequently uses the phrase *ez īn jānib*, characteristic of popular works but not used by Neshrī, and his sentences frequently run on with a string of verbs in *-ub* and several changes of subject, a loose construction to which Neshrī is not addicted. Again, unlike Neshrī, he notes numerous appointments, deaths, and dismissals, not only of prominent statesmen but of local officials whom he knew, and also records visitations of the plague in the cities in which he found himself.

The strongest argument against Neshrī's authorship is the autobiographical matter. Neshrī's one authentic reference to himself, as *bīčāre* (*Mz* 219, 8/*Mn* 309, 16), the redactor reproduces (fol. 75^r) in the words *bu kitāb mü'ellifi*; the later autobiographical references, however, are all to '*faḳīr*'. Some details of the notes given in the continuation remain obscure to me, for the writer

[1] Pb fol. 4^r (= *Ank* 14, 19, variant not listed).

[2] e.g. apparatus to *Ank* 16, 4; 18, 6 and 12.

[3] The notices on the 'ulemā are distributed through the text at the ends of the appropriate reigns, see apparatus to *Ank* 148, 3 and 186, 4.

switches without warning from local to national matters, he is sometimes confused in his chronology, and in referring to his own affairs he sometimes contents himself with an allusion. However, his career seems to run thus:[1]

Early in 897, on being appointed *khaṭīb* for the village of Delüler near Alashehir,[2] he went to Istanbul (presumably to obtain his writ of appointment [*berāt*]), where he stayed for some time; from there he went on a visit to Izmir, where he arrived on 1 Rejeb [898?]. He then became a *kātib* (perhaps to the ḳāḍī of Izmir), visiting Istanbul in Dhu 'l-Ḥijja 898 to collect his *berāt*. He got married a year later, in Muḥarrem 900; he is evidently still at Izmir, for he notes the arrival there of the beylerbey of Anadolu, Hersek-zāde Aḥmed Pasha, on a tour of inspection, in Jumādā II 901. In Dhu 'l-Ḳa'de 902 he became *imām* of 'Alā'iyya. In Dhu 'l-Ḳa'de 904 he went to Edirne, again apparently to collect a *berāt*, for an appointment at the '*'imāret* of Juneyd Beg'—evidently a return to Izmir, where this *'imāret* was.[3] In Rebī' II 907 he received a *berāt* as *türbedār* from the newly-appointed ḳāḍī'asker Mü'eyyedzāde: he is still at Izmir, for he notes the arrival there of Kemāl Re'īs's fleet, driven from Lesbos by the Franco-Venetian expedition in that year. In Dhu 'l-Ḳa'de of the same year he was reappointed *imām* of 'Alā'iyya, receiving his *berāt* at Üsküdar. He notes the death in Sha'bān 910 of a certain 'Abdurraḥmān b. Khāṣṣbegi, whose funeral-prayer he himself led, and records the birth of 'Memi Khoja' (his own son?) on Thursday, 19 Rebī' II 911. He had by then left 'Alā'iyya, and in Dhu 'l-Ḥijja of that year went to Istanbul again, apparently for a new *berāt*, for in that month he became *kātib* and *khaṭīb* of Koz-aghač: this would appear to be the village of that name 8 km. north of Muğla, for he records immediately the appointment of a new ḳāḍī to the not-so-distant Izmir. At the end of Ramażān 918, after the accession of Selīm I, his *berāt* was renewed; he is still somewhere near Ma'nīsa, for he speaks of Selīm 'coming' there in pursuit of Korkud, and notes appointments at Ma'nīsa and Tire as late as 922/1516.[4]

[1] The relevant passages of Pb are quoted in Appendix V, pp. 82–84.
[2] Modern maps show the village Deliler some 13 km. east of Alashehir.
[3] See Himmet Akın, *Aydın Oğulları tarihi hakkında bir araştırma*, Istanbul, 1946, 70.
[4] The redactor's interest in the Aydın district is shown also by insertions at earlier points in the text, see apparatus to *Ank* 166, 16; 204, 16–17.

This is the career of a young man. He appears first in 897/1492 as *khaṭīb* in a small village, gets married in 900/1494, and rises to be *imām* of 'Alā'iyya in 902/1497. Neshrī, however, eleven years before the date of this first appointment and already of mature age, had been in the camp when Meḥemmed II died. Again, if the continuator is Neshrī himself, why should he be so reticent about his own affairs before 897 and then suddenly introduce this series of autobiographical notes?

The text contained in MSS. Pb and D is the work of a humble, anonymous cleric. Its continuation certainly deserves publication, if only for the many precise dates which it gives; but it cannot be the work of the still more shadowy historian we know as Neshrī.

Supplementary Note. While these pages were in the press, Professor Inalcık, with his customary kindness, sent me a microfilm of the continuation found in MS. D. It is not related, I find, to that in MS. Pb but is identical with that in MS. V (see p. 52, above); it ends with almost the same words, even to Furūshī's chronogram for A.H. 1066 (see *Mz* (*Einl.*) 21). MS. Pb, with its autobiographical references, therefore stands alone.

APPENDIX I

CONCORDANCE OF TEXTS AND SOURCES

THE first four columns are a concordance for the contents of Taeschner's facsimile edition of the Codex Menzel (*Mz*), the two volumes (with continuous pagination) of the Turkish printed text (*Ank*), the Vienna MS. (W), and the *Historiae musulmanae* (*H.M.*). W is included in order to facilitate reference to Wittek's *Quellenproblem.* Parallel passages in the facsimile edition of the Codex Manisa (*Mn*) can be identified immediately through the *Mz* and W page-references in its margins.

Each entry for *Mz*, *Ank*, and W is to be understood as 'chapter whose heading appears at p. —'; when two or more headings appear on a page, they are distinguished as 'a', 'b' (i.e. 'first, second heading'), &c., line-references being given only when a heading is lacking or not quickly recognizable. References to *H.M.* are to be understood 'reproduced in the section beginning at column —, line —', the reference for the end of the section being given only when Leunclavius there digresses from Han. or follows an order different from Neshrī's.

The remaining columns are an indication of the sources which Neshrī was using for each chapter. The references for ʿĀpz are to the chapter-numbers (*bāb*) of Giese's edition (Neshrī's readings are in general closest to the ʿĀpz MS. M). The references to O.A. (MS. Marsh 313) indicate that Neshrī is following his 'second source' for material found at these pages of O.A., an asterisk signifying that O.A.'s account is briefer than (but recognizably related to) that which Neshrī used. The references to the chronological list are to event(s) recorded in the lists for A.H. 856 and 858 (quoted in Appendix III) under 'retrospective' dates which, re-computed, indicate these Hijra years.

The sign = does not necessarily indicate that Neshrī's and the source's accounts agree verbatim, but merely that there is no necessity to postulate that Neshrī was using a further written source; × indicates 'harmonized, conflated with'; + indicates 'appended'.

Not all the dates which Neshrī assigns to events are to be explained from these three sources: in his early chapters Neshrī is fitting the legendary tales of the origin of the Ottomans into the framework of contemporary political history, and for later ones his list probably provided a slightly different chronology from that of the extant lists.

THIRD *ṬABAḲA*, TO THE DEATH OF 'OSMĀN GHĀZĪ

	Mz	*Ank*	MS. W	*H.M.*	*'Āpz*	O.A.
1	18, 19	54a	17^v		[introductory]	
2	19a	54b	17^v	cf. 89, 48–90, 21		14^v–15^r[1]
3	19b	56	18^v	cf. 92, 32–48, & 94, 49–97, 5	§2 to p. 6, 8	× 14^v
4	20, 10	60	19^v	97, 6–51, & 98, 21–100, 48	§2, p. 6, 8–7, 12 [+relation of Mevlānā Ayās][3]	× 15^{r}–^{v}, 16^v,[2] 17^r
5	22a	64	21^r	100, 48	§6	× 17^{r}–^{v}
6	22b	66	21^r	101, 47	§7	× 18^r
7[4]	23a	70	22^r	103, 11–105, 21	[contemporary political history]	
8	23, 16	72, 12	23^r	105, 21–106, 9		
	24, 3	72, 2	22^v	107, 14–49		
9	24, 7	74	23^v	107, 49–110, 53		
10	25a	78a	24^v	111, 10–19, & 112, 1–54		
11	25b	78b	25^r	122, 48–124, 17	= §3	
12	25c	80	25^v	113, 24–115, 15	= §4	
13	26	84	26^v	124, 17	§5, §8; p. 13, n. 4; p. 203, 12–13	
14	27, 9	86	27^v	126, 34	= §9	
15	27, 21	88	28^v	128, 39	= §10	
16	28	92	29^v	131, 7		
17	29	94	30^v	132, 37	= §11	
18	30	96	31^r	134, 10	= §12	
19	31	102	33^r	138, 25–49	= §13	
20	32	104	33^v	139, 6–140, 48, & 148, 34–151, 20	(echoes of §§ 8, 14)	O.A. has lost some leaves after f. 20
21	33	110	35^v	152, 23	= §15	
22	34a	112	36^r	154, 6	= §16	
23	34b	114	36^v	155, 45–158, 15	= §17	
24	35a	116	38^r	158, 23	= §§ 18–19	
25	35b	118	38^r	159, 13	= §20	
26	36a	122	39^v	162, 30	= §21	
27	36b	124	40^r	163, 23–166, 25, & 166, 33–167, 37	= §22	
28	38	128	42^r	167, 37–171, 49, 173, 19–24, & 174, 1–34	= §23	
29	40a	144, 13	47^r	175, 13–176, 22	= §24	
30	40b	144, 4	47^r	173, 29–54, & 175, 10–13	[tradition?]	
31	40c	136	44^v	181, 47	= §25	
32	41	138	45^r	184, 6	= §26	
33	42a	142a	46^v	185, 47–186, 16	= §27	
34	42b	72, 8	23^r	176, 22–33	= p. 193, 10–12	
35	42c	142b	46^v	174, 34–175, 1	= §28	

[1] Neshrī harmonizes the genealogy found in O.A. with that given in his first *ṭabaḳa*, *Mz* 5, 4/ *Ank* 10, 6–7.

[2] The text of O.A. fols. 16^v, 6–17^r, 11 is quoted in Appendix II.

[3] Mz has a further genealogy for Ertoghrul, see p. 37.

[4] The chapters numbered 7–10 comprise the 'first block' and those numbered 28–34 the 'second block', whose order is discussed at pp. 25–27.

REIGN OF ORKHĀN

	Mz	*Ank*	MS. W	*H.M.*	*'Āpz*	O.A.
1	42d	146	47^{v}	177, 5–179, 5	= §29	
2	43	148	48^{v}	186, 17–188, 15, & 190, 34–191, 23	= §30	
3	44	152	49^{v}	191, 26–192, 46	= §31 to p. 37, 18	
4	45a	156, 2	50^{v}	192, 46	= §31 from p. 37, 19	
5	45b	156	51^{r}	193, 17–194, 45	= §32	
6	46a	162a	51^{v}	195, 3	= §33	
7	46b	162b	52^{r}	195, 45	= §34	
8	46c	164	52^{r}	196, 36	= §35	
9	47a	166a	53^{r}	198, 18	= §36	
10	47b	166b	53^{r}	198, 45	= §37	
11	47c	166c	53^{v}	199, 1–201, 23	= §38	
12	48	170	54^{v}	205, 17	§39	× *21^{r}–22^{r}, 23^{r}
13	50a	180	56^{v}	209, 18	= §40	
14	50b	182	57^{r}	210, 13	§41[1]	
15	51a	184	58^{r}	211, 42–212, 22	§42	× 24^{v}
16	51b	186	58^{v}	215, 4–216, 30	p. 193, 13–16	× *21^{r}

[1] Modified by Neshrī, probably under the influence of his chronological list, see p. 43 and n. 2.

REIGN OF MURĀD I

	Mz	*Ank*	MS. W	*H.M.*	*'Āpz*	O.A.
1	52	190	59^{r}	217, 5	§43[1]	× *26^{r-v}
2	53a	192	60^{r}	220, 37	= §44	
3	53b	194	60^{v}	221, 26–222, 7	= §45	
4	53c	196	61^{r}	227, 14	= §46	
5	54a	198	62^{r}	228, 54	= §47	
6	54b	200	62^{r}	229, 32–230, 27	= §48	
7	55a	202a	62^{v}	231, 21–53, & 234, 13–36	= §49	
8	55b	202b	63^{r}	234, 37	= §50	
9	56a	204	63^{v}	235, 52	= §51	
10	56b	206	64^{v}	237, 15	= §52	
11	57a	208	65^{r}	238, 29–239, 2	= §53	
12	57b	210a	65^{r}	239, 14	§54 to p. 55, 7	× 26^{v}–27^{r}
13	57c	210b	65^{v}	239, 43–242, 3	+§54 from p. 55, 7	*27^{r-v}
14	58a	214a	66^{v}	242, 10–23, & 243, 48–244, 19	§55	× 29^{v}
15	58b	214b	67^{r}	244, 50		
16	59, 7	216	67^{v}	246, 20		
17	59	218	68^{r}	247, 7		
18	60a	220a	68^{v}	248, 38		
19	60b	220b	69^{r}	249, 12		
20	61	224	70^{v}	252, 34		
21	62	226	70^{v}	253, 28		
22	63	230	72^{r}	255, 47		
23	63, 16	232	72^{r}	256, 17–258, 20		
24	64	234	72^{v}	259, 8		
25	64, 20	236a	73^{r}	261, 51		
26	65a	236b	73^{v}	262, 20		
27	65b	238	73^{v}	262, 45		
28	66a	242	74^{v}	266, 11–267, 5		
29	66b	244a	75^{r}	268, 33		
30	67	244b	75^{v}	269, 15		
31	67, 18	246	76^{r}	270, 35		
32	68a	248a	76^{v}	271, 46		
33	68b	248b	77^{r}	272, 13		
34	69a	250	77^{r}	273, 16		
35	69b	252	78^{r}	274, 24		
36	69c	254	78^{v}	275, 18		
37	70a	256a	79^{r}	276, 47		
38	70b	256b	79^{v}	277, 1		
39	71a	258a	79^{v}	277, 25		
40	71b	258b	80^{r}	278, 7		
41	72a	260	80^{v}	279, 31		
42	72b	262	81^{r}	280, 42		
43	72c	264	81^{v}	282, 4		
44	73a	266	82^{r}	283, 1		
45	73b	268	82^{v}	283, 20		
46	74	270	83^{r}	284, 36		
47	75a	272	83^{v}	286, 23		

Neshrī's chapters 15–57 reproduce the account of his 'second source', of which only a much abridged version is given in O.A., fols. 27^{v}–34^{r}.

[1] On the authority of his chronological list Neshrī ascribes the conquest of Gelibolu to Murād I, cf. Appendix III, sub anno [755].

	Mz	*Ank*	MS. W	*H.M.*	*'Āpz*	O.A.
48	75b	274a	84^r	287, 17		
49	75c	274b	84^v	287, 52		
50	76a	276	85^r	288, 35		
51	76b	278	85^v	289, 34		
52	78	284	87^r	293, 24		
53	78, 19	286	88^r	294, 26		
54	79	288	88^v	295, 7		
55	80a	292	89^v	297, 21		
56	80b	294	90^v	298, 16–301, 16		
57	82a	302, 15	92^r			
58	82b	304	92^v	301, 17–302, 44	+§57 from p. 58, 4, p. 203, 2 & 20–21	*34^{r-v}
59	83	306	93^r	304, 31–306, 31	+p. 193, 18–20	*25^v–26^r

REIGN OF BĀYEZĪD I

	Mz	*Ank*	MS. W	*H.M.*	*'Āpz*	O.A.
1	84a	310	94^{r}	315, 4	§58	$\times 35^{r}$
2	84b	312	94^{v}	316, 3	= §59	
3	85a	314	95^{r}	318, 8	§64	
4	85b	316a	95^{v}	319, 24–320, 15		= 35^{v}–36^{v}
5	86	316b	96^{r}	332, 50	p. 65, 6, p. 66, 3–9	$\times 36^{v}$–38^{v}[1]
6	87	320	97^{v}	335, 28–336, 26	§65	$\times 38^{v}$–39^{r}[2]
7	88a	322	98^{r}	320, 21		= 39^{r-v}[2]
8	88b	324	98^{r}	320, 46	§60	$\times 39^{v}$–41^{v}
9	90a	328	99^{v}	324, 6	= §61	
10	90b	330a	100^{r}	325, 25	= §62	
11	90c	330b	100^{v}	325, 42–326, 28	= §63	
12	91	332	100^{v}	336, 27–337, 51	cf. p. 66, 9–12	*41^{v}–44^{r}
13	92a	336, 4	101^{v}		= §63, *Laṭīfe*	
14	92b	338	102^{v}	337, 52	= §67 to p. 67, 3	
15	93a	340	102^{v}	338, 17–53	= §67, *su'āl* at p. 67, 9	
16	93b	342	103^{r}	342, 34	§67, *su'āl* at p. 67, 15	$\times 43^{v}$
17	94	346	104^{r}	345, 17	§67, from p. 69, 8	$\times 44^{r}$
18	95	348	105^{r}	346, 33–350, 41	§67, from p. 69, 22	× *44^{v}, 45^{v}
19	97a	356	107^{r}	350, 42–351, 20, & 339, 43–340, 14	= §67, from p. 71, 23	
20	97b	358	107^{v}	340, 15	{[relation of Ḳuṭbeddīn-oghlu] +§67, p. 72, 6–11	
21	97c	360a	108^{v}	340, 51–342, 12	§58 & p. 193, 21–23	× *42^{v}

[1] Neshrī is here influenced by his list, cf. Appendix III, sub annis [799] and [801].
[2] These passages are quoted in Appendix II.

THE INTERREGNUM

	Mz	*Ank*	MS. W	*H.M.*	*'Āpz*	O.A.
1	98a	364a	108^{v}	371, 7–42	§68 to p. 72, 21	× *46^{r}
2	98b	364b	109^{r}		= p. 72, 21–p. 73, 1	
3	98c	366	109^{r}	372, 38		= 46^{v}–
4	99	368	110^{r}	374, 12		= 47^{v}–
5	100	372	111^{r}	376, 32		= 49^{r}–
6	102a	378	112^{v}	378, 49		= 51^{r}–
7	102b	380	113^{r}	379, 29		= 52^{r}–
8	104	386	115^{r}	382, 17		= 54^{v}–
9	107	394	117^{v}	386, 44		= 58^{v}–
10	109a	400	119^{r}	389, 7		= 60^{r}–
11	109b	402	120^{r}	390, 11		= 61^{r}–
12	111	406	121^{r}	392, 17		= 62^{v}–
13	112	412	122^{v}	394, 45		= 64^{v}–
14	113	416	123^{v}	396, 17		= 65^{v}–
15	114	422	124^{v}	398, 11–47, & 399, 43–		= 67^{r}–
16	115	424	125^{v}	401, 39		= 68^{r}–
17	116	428	126^{v}	403, 51		= 70^{r}–
18	117	430	127^{v}	405, 26		= 71^{r}–
19	118	436	129^{r}	408, 38		= 73^{r}–
20	119	440	130^{r}	409, 46		= 74^{r}–
21	121	444	131^{v}	412, 27–416, 23		= 76^{v}–
22	123	450	133^{v}	420, 11		= 79^{r}–
23	124	454	134^{v}	422, 44		= 80^{v}–
24	125	460	136^{r}	425, 13		= 82^{v}–
25	128	468	138^{v}	429, 52		= 85^{v}–
26	129	472	139^{v}	431, 26		= 87^{r}–
27	130a	476	140^{r}	432, 50		= 88^{r}–
28	130b	480a	141^{r}	434, 29		= 89^{v}
29	131	480b	141^{v}	435, 6–438, 53		= 89^{v}–
30	133a	486	143^{v}	446, 4		= 92^{r}–
31	133b	490	144^{r}	446, 43		= 92^{v}–
32	135	496	145^{v}	449, 53		= 95^{r}–
33	136	502	147^{r}	452, 39–460, 52		= 97^{r}–103^{r}

REIGN OF MEḤEMMED I

	Mz	*Ank*	MS. W	*H.M.*	*'Āpz*	O.A.	List
1	141a	516a	151^{v}	—	[cf. Shukrullāh 106, 6]		
2	141b	516b	151^{v}	468, 40	§71	[cf. Shukrullāh 104, 22][1]	
3	142	524	153^{v}	470, 34	= §72		
4	143a	526	154^{r}	471, 33	= §73		
5	143b	528	154^{v}	472, 22	§74		× [818] [819]
6	143c	534	156^{v}	473, 24	§75	× *105^{r}–106^{r}	× [820] [822] [823]
7	145a	540	158^{r}	476, 1	= §76		
8	145b	542a	158^{v}	477, 1	= §77		
9	146	542b	158^{v}	477, 43	= §§78–79 & p. 75, 14–15		
10	147a	546	160^{r}	479, 32	= §80		
11	147b	550a	160^{v}	480, 18	= p. 194, 1–4		
12	147c	550b	160^{v}	480, 44–484, 4	§81	× *160^{r}	
						[cf. Shukrullāh 112, 4 ff.]	

[1] Neshrī's other additions may reflect local tradition in Bursa, see pp. 18–19, above.

REIGN OF MURĀD II

	Mz	*Ank*	MS. W.	*H.M.*	*'Āpz*	O.A.	List
1	148	554	162^{r}	483, 26	§82 & p. 84, 6	[cf. Shukrullāh 112, 6]	+[824]
2	149a	556	162^{v}	484, 30	= §83		
3	149b	558	163^{r}	486, 6	= §84		
4	150	560	163^{v}	487, 19	= §85		
5	151a	562	164^{r}	488, 35–490, 18	= §86		
					§87	× 108^{v}–109^{r}	
6	151b	566a	165^{r}	523, 31	= §88		
7	152a	566b	165^{v}	524, 35	= §89		
8	152b	570	166^{v}	526, 20	§90	× *110^{r}	+[826]
	—	572	167^{r}	—	[interpolation, see p. 50]		
9	153	574	167^{v}	527, 30	= §§91–92		
10	154a	578a	168^{v}	529, 5	= §93		
11	154b	578b	168^{v}	529, 38	§94 to p. 94, 24		?+[828]
12	155a	580	169^{r}	530, 37	= §94, *su'āl*		
13	155b	582a	169^{v}	531, 5	= §95		
14	156	582b	170^{r}	532, 8	= §96		
15	157a	586	171^{r}	533, 47	= §97		
16	157b	590	172^{r}	535, 35	§98	× 111^{v}	+[830]
17	158	592	172^{v}	536, 34	= §99		
18	159	598	174^{r}	539, 4	= §100		
19	160a	600	175^{r}	540, 1	= §101		
20	160b	602	175^{v}	540, 42	= §102		
21	161a	604	175^{v}	541, 17	= §103		
22	161b	606	176^{v}	542, 17	§104		+[833]
23	162	610	177^{v}	544, 19	§105		+[833], [834]
24	163	612	178^{v}	545, 38	= §106		
25	165a	616	179^{v}	547, 44	§107	× 113^{r}	+[839]
26	165b	618	180^{r}	548, 40	= §108		
27	166a	620	180^{v}	549, 26	= §109		
28	166b	622	181^{r}	550, 6	§110	× 113^{v}	
29	167a	624a	181^{v}	550, 49	= §111		
30	167b	624b	182^{r}	551, 34	= §112		
31	167c	626	182^{r}	552, 4	§113	× 114^{r-v}	+[842]
32	169	630	183^{v}	554, 24	§114		+[844]
33	170a	634	184^{v}	555, 40	§115 to p. 118, 10		×[845]
34	170b	636	185^{v}	556, 35	§115 from p. 118, 10, & §116		×[846]
35	171	644	186^{r}	558, 12	§117 to p. 120, 17	× 114^{v}–115^{r}	×[847]
36	172a	646	187^{r}	559, 38	§117 from p. 120, 18	× 115^{v}	
37	172b	648	187^{v}	560, 17	§118	× 118^{r}–119^{v}	
38	174a	656	190^{r}	564, 36	= §119 to p. 123, 15		
39	174b	658, 6	190^{v}	565, 10	= §119 from p. 123, 15		
40	174c	658	190^{v}	565, 24	= §120		
41	176	674	192^{r}	568, 30	= §121		
42	177a	676	193^{r}	569, 32	p. 194, 5–10	× 120^{r-v}	
43	177b	680	193^{v}	570, 44–574, 4	§122 to p. 130, 9, & p. 129, 13–14	[cf. Shukrullāh 118, 1–13]	

REIGN OF MEḤEMMED II

	Mz	*Ank*	MS. W.	*H.M.*	*'Āpz*	O.A.
1	178a	682	194r	575, 23	p. 129, 14[1]	
2	178b	684	194v	575, 31	§ 122 from p. 130, 9	× 124v–125v
3	179	686	195r	577, 26	§ 123 to p. 133, 4	× 126r–v
4	180	688	195v	578, 16	§ 123 from p. 133, 4	× 127r–v, 128v[2]
5	181a	708	196v	580, 21	= § 124	
6	181b	710	197r	581, 27–582, 35	§ 124 from p. 137, 8, & p. 195, 1–7[3]	
7	182	712	198r		= § 125	
8	183a	716	198v			= 129r–131r,[4] 132r
9	183b	718	199v		§ 126	× 131v
10	184	720	200v		§ 127	× 135r–136r
11	185	724	201v		= § 128	
12	186, 17	728	202v		§ 129 to p. 132, 4	× 137r–138r
13	187	730	203r		§ 129 from p. 132, 4	× 137r, 138v–139r
14	188	732b	204r		= § 130	
15	189a	736	204v		§ 131	× 138v
16	189b	738	205v		§ 132	× 139r
17	190	740	206v		= § 133	
18	192	746a	208v		= § 134	
19	193a	748	209r		= § 135	
20	193b	750	210r		= § 136	
21	195	754	211r		= §§ 137–8	
22	196a	758	212r		= § 139	

[*continued overleaf*

1 Neshrī gives further a precise date for Meḥemmed's birth, not found in the sources.
2 Neshrī gives further (*Mz* 180, 15) precise dates for the beginning and end of the siege of Constantinople, not found in the sources.
3 Neshrī has extra details, presumably from personal knowledge.
4 The beginning of this passage is quoted in Appendix II.

REIGN OF MEḤEMMED II (*cont.*)

	Mz	*Ank*	MS. W	*ʿĀpz*	O.A.
23	196b	760	212^{v}	§ 140	× 144^{r}–145^{v}
24	199a	766	215^{r}		= 145^{v}–146^{v}
25	199b	768a	215^{v}		= 146^{v}–147^{r}
26	199c	768b	215^{v}		= 147^{r}–148^{r}
27	200	770	216^{v}	§ 141[1]	
28	201	776	218^{r}	§ 142	× 148^{r-v}
29	202a	778a	218^{v}		= 148^{v}–149^{r}
30	202b	778b	218^{v}	§ 143	× 151^{v}[1]
31	203a	784a	220^{r}		= 152^{r-v}
32	203b	784b	220^{r}	§ 144	× 154^{r}
33	204	788	221^{r}	= § 145	
34	205a	790	221^{v}	§ 146[1]	
35	205b	792	222^{r}	= § 147 to p. 167, 17	
36	206a	794	222^{v}	= § 147 from p. 167, 18	
37	206b	796	223^{r}	§ 148[1]	
38	207	798	223^{v}	§ 149[1]	
39	208	802	224^{v}	§ 150 to p. 171, 18	× 154^{v}–155^{v}
40	209	808	226^{r}	§ 150 from p. 171, 18[2]	
41	210a	810	226^{v}	[relation of ʿOmer Beg]	
42	210b	812	227^{r}	§ 151 to p. 174, 3[2]	
43	212a	818a	228^{v}	§ 151, p. 174, 9–14[2]	
44	212b	818b	229^{r}	§ 151, p. 174, 15–19[2]	
45	212c	820	229^{v}	§ 151 from p. 175, 3	× 133^{v}[3]
46	213	822	229^{v}	= § 152 to p. 177, 6	
47	214	826	231^{v}	= § 152 from p. 177, 6	[+chronogram]
48	215a	828a	231^{v}	§ 153 to p. 178, 19	× 134^{r}
49	215b	828b	232^{r}	= § 153 from p. 178, 19	
50	216a	832	232^{v}	= § 154	
51	216b	834	233^{r}	= § 155	
52	217	838a	234^{v}	[personal knowledge?]	
53	218a	838b	235^{r}		
54	218b	840	235^{v}	§ 156[4]	
55	219a	842	236^{r}	[chronogram]	
56	219b		236^{r}	= § 157 to p. 183, 1 [+Neshrī's own relation]	

[1] Extra details on events in Karaman may be from Neshrī's personal knowledge, see p. 18.
[2] Extra details are presumably from ʿOmer Beg's relation of the campaign.
[3] Fols. 133–4 are mis-bound in the manuscript: they should follow fol. 157.
[4] Neshrī has extra details, presumably from personal knowledge.

REIGN OF BĀYEZĪD II[1]

	Mz	MS. W	*'Āpz*	O.A.
1	220	237^{v}	§§ 158–9	× 163^{r-v}
2	221	238	§ 160	× 164^{r}
3	222	239^{v}	§ 161	× 164^{v}–165^{r}
4	223	240^{r}	§ 162	× 165^{r}–167^{v}[2]
5	225	241^{v}	= § 163	
6	226	243^{r}	= § 164	
7	227	243^{r}	= § 165	
8	228a	244^{v}	= § 167 [works of Bāyezīd II]	
9	228b	245^{r}	= § 168 [summary-chapter on vezirs]	
10	232, 2	248^{r}	= § 169 [summary-chapter on 'ulemā]	
11	233, 9	249^{v}	= § 167 [works of Bāyezīd II, repeated]	
12	233, 18	250^{r}	[Ḳaṣīde]	

[1] In some of these chapters appear details not found in the sources, which Neshrī has presumably added from personal knowledge.
[2] The last part of this passage is quoted in Appendix II.

APPENDIX II

SPECIMENS OF THE TEXT OF O.A.
(MS. MARSH 313)

I. From the author's preface (fol. 4$^{\text{r–v}}$), cf. pp. 11–12, above.
II. Ertoghrul in the service of Sultan ʿAlāeddīn (fols. 16^{v}–17^{r}), cf. *Mz* 20, 15; 21, 9–10; 22, 3–7.
III. Bāyezīd I's campaigns against Kastamuni and Selanik (fols. 38^{v}–39^{v}), cf. *Mz* 87, 17–88, 13.
IV. Meḥemmed II's Serbian campaign of 858/1454 (fols. 129^{r}–130^{r}), cf. *Mz* 183, 7–15.
V. Bāyezīd II's conquest of Akkerman (fol. 166^{v}–end), cf. *Mz* 224, 1–22.

(A few slips in the text are tacitly corrected.)

I

وچون بو بندهٔ ضعیف قلیل البضاعه که اباً عن جد اول خاندان شریف نعمتیله پرورده اولمشدر سعادت مساعدت ودولت معاونت ایدوب اول پادشاه کریمك شرف خذمتیله مشرّف اولب سلك خدام وعبیدنده منسلك اولمق میسّر اولدی الحمد لله والمنّه بعض محاورات شریفه‌لری اثناسنده بو معنی فهم اولندی که تواریخ سلاطین اولی الامر اسلامیّه که جناب حق جلّ وعلادن ایجاب اطاعتده تالی رسول واقع اولمشلردی بعد قصص الانبیا احسن قصص کورنور بو جهتدن‌درکه اکابر علما انوك ضبطنه وتحریرنه ملتزم اولب اول بابده کتابلر تصنیف اتمشلردر امّا تواریخ اشرف سلاطین که ال عثماندر عبارات عامّ النفع ایله کما ینبغی جمع اولمامشدر اولسه مستحسن ادی بو بندهٔ حقیر معنای مذکوره اطلاع باعث اولدیکه اول تواریخِ عبارات ترکیّه ایله که دیار رومده عام اَلنفع‌در جمع ایده

پس بو کتابده سلاطین علیّهٔ عثمانیّه ابّدهم الله بالسلطنة الی یوم القیام حکایتلرندن معلوم اولنلروك صحیحلری علی وجه الاختصار تدوین اولندی امیذدر که اول عالی درکاهده مهبّ قبول واقع اولب عین رضایله ملحوظ اولا

II

سلطان علاء الدین بر اثناده غزا نیّتنه لشکر جمع ادوب قونیه‌دن قالقوب کونلردن بر کون سلطان ایوکنه قونمشدی مکر عیص اولادندن ارطوکرل سلطان علاء الدینوك غزایه کتدوکن ایشدوب جمله جماعتیله کوجمال قالقوب کلوب سلطان ایوکنده سلطان علاء الدین خذمتنه یتشوب مقدارنجه پیش‌کش چکوب سلطان بونی خیلی خوشچه کورب اقنجی‌باشی قلدی ارطوکرلوك اوج اوغلی واردی بری عثمان وبری کوندوز وبری صارویاتی که اکا سوجی داخی درلردی ارطوکرل اوغلی صارویاتی سلطان علیء الدینه کوندردیکه بزه داخی یورت کوستروك دیدیلر سلطان داخی بونلروك کلماسندن بغایت فرح اولب قرجه حصار تکوری وبلجوك تکوری سلطانه مطیع اولب خراج ویررلردی اول اکی حصارك ارالغی کم سکوتدر انی یورت کوستردیلر اول زمانده کوتاهیّه بل‌که تمام کرمیان ایلی هنوز دار الحرب ایدی ارطوکرل چون چری باشی اولب چری چکوب خیلی کویلر وکندلر اورب وایللر غارت ایدوب باش باش دری کافرلر ومال غنیمتلر کتوره باشلدی اول سببدن سلطان علاء الدین اقدام تام ادوب صاحبك قرا حصاری اوزرنه دُشوب قره حصاری محاصره ادوب قبله طرفنه ارطوکرلِ قودی

III

پادشاه اسلام قسطمونیی وسلانیکی فتح اتدکیدر

چون اوّل بهار اولب تاریخ هجرت یدی یوز طقسان بشنجی ییلده پادشاه اسلام اهل عسکره خبر ایدوب اناطولی وروم ایلی عسکرن جمع ایدوب یوریوب قسطمونیه اوزرنه هجوم ایدجك کوترم بایزید داخی فوت اولب قسطمونیه وعثمانچق وجانیك وصامصون فتح اولندی هم اول تاریخده تکه وکرمیان ولایتلری تمام تعلقاتلریله فتح اولنوب اندن قره حصار وبك شهری وسیدی شهری فتح اولنوب اولولری پایهٔ سریر اعلایه کلوب قلعه‌لرن تسلیم ایدوب خلعت کیوب منصبلر الوب یرلرنه روانه اولدیلر قسطمونیّه ولایتن اوغلی امیر سَلْمانه باغشلیوب منتشا اوغلی اندن قاچوب چغتایه کتدی اندن پادشاه اسلام سالماً وغانماً کلوب محروسهٔ بروساده عدل وداد اتمکه مشغول اولب عیش ونوش ایدرکن خبر کلدیکه فرنك ملعون کمبیله کناره چقوب خیلی ایل غارت ایدوب روم ایلنده دکیز کنارلری محکم فترات‌در دنلجك پادشاه عالم‌پناه داخی بهار اولمادن یاننده اولان عسکریله یوریوب روم ایلنه کچوب انده روم ایلی عسکرن جمع ایدوب سلانیك اوزرنه متوجّه اولدی بی محابا مجال ورمیوب انی فتح ایدوب اول کنارده اولان مسلمانلردن خیلی اولر کتوروب حصارك ایچین طولدردی اندن یوریوب یکی‌شهره واثنه‌یه واروب اول کنارده اولان حصارلری فتح ایدوب عسکر خلقی بر وجهله غنیمت تحصیل اتدیلر که قابل وصف اولمیوب سالماً وغانماً مقرّ مالوف‌لرنه عودت اتدیلر سلانیك فتح اولندغی هجرتوك یدی یوز طقسان التنجی ییلوك جماذی الاخرنك اون طقزنجی کوننده واقع اولدی اندن پادشاه اسلام

دولت وسعادتله کلوب بروساده متمکّن اولب فرنکله تمام عداوت ایدوب اطراف وجوانبه مکتوبلر ارسال اتدی

IV

پاذشاه اسلام لاز ایلی وسفریجه حصاری واُمول قلعه‌سین فتح اتدکی‌در

چون پاذشاه اسلام استانبول امرندن فراغت ایدوب ادرنده متمکّن اولب اطراف وجوانبدن کلان ایلچیلره دستور ورمشدی مکر ولق اوغلنوك ایلچسی انده حاضر اولب عسکر جرارك بو وجهله مهابتن وصلابتن وقلعهٔ نیجه فتح اتدکارنی کوروب ولق اوغلنه خبر ورمشدی ولق اوغلی داخی مرحوم سلطان مراد وفات اتدکی وقت لاز ایلنوك بعضن کیرو الوب قبض اتمشدی استانبول فتح اولدوغن ایشدجك مجموعین پاذشاهَ تسلیم اتمشدی امّا قلبنده کیرو کین طوتب اهل اسلامدن بعض یولجیلری غافل بولدقلری یرده هلاك ایدرلردی حتی لاز ایلندن اُسکوبه یول قالمیوب منقطع اولمشدی پرشتنه‌ده بر قاضی واردی خیلی مُسُلمان وصالح کمسنه ایدی کافروك بو افعالنه مطّلع اولب پاذشاه اسلامه مکتوب کوندرب عرض اتمشدی پاذشاه اسلام داخی ولق اوغلنه بر یرار قولین کوندروب بو خبروك اصلی ندر دیو استفسار ایدجك ولق اوغلی پاذشاه قولنه التفات اتمیوب عناد وتمرّد ایدوب عداوت اظهار اتدی پس قضیّه بو وجهله اولیجق تفاصیلیله قول داخی پاذشاه اسلامه عرض اتدی هماندم پاذشاه داخی ادرنده عسکر جمع ایدوب بر وجه استعجال الجه حصاره متوجّه اولدی وروم ایلنوك اقنجی‌لرنه امر ایتدی ولق ایلن غارت اتدیلر ولق اوغلی بو خبری ایشدجك منفعل اولب اتدکی اشلره پشیمان اولب نیجه

ایده‌جکین بلمیوب ایللرنه آدم کوندروب متموّل کافرلری اسبابلریله سوریجه حصاره طولدردی پاذشاه داخی طغرو سمندرنوك ازرنه واروب اراقدن بر نوبت جنك ایدوب حصاردن داخی کافر چقوب برز جنك اولب کافری کیرو حصاره قویدیلر پاذشاه اسلام انده قونمایوب هماندم سوریجه حصاره توجّه اندی وولق اوغلی قاچوب انکروسه کتدی

V

اندن صکره سلطان مذکور قلعه‌نوك خرابین عسکرنه امر ایدوب فی الحال تعمیر ایدوب والات حربلرن واسبابلرن مرتّب ومکمّل اتدروب اندن صکره جماذی الآخروك یکرمِ بشنجی کون کلی ازرندن عنان عزیمتی دولت واقبال برله اقکرمانَ قلعه‌سی ازرنه مصمّم ایدب کوج بر کوج ایدوب دُردنجی کونده قلعه‌نوك ازرنه دوشب اللّی بیك مقداری تاتار عسکریله اول اراده یولداشلق ایچون کلوب سلطان خدمتنه یتشدی واق کرمان ازرنده اون بیش کون اکی جانبدن اوقله وطوپ توفکله محکم جنك اولب آخر الامر سنهٔ مذکور رجبنوك اون اکنجی کونِ محکم محاربه اولب قلعه خندقنوك یدی وسکز قولاج عرضی وعمقی اولب صارپلقده غایتده اولمسی برله خراب ویباب قلوب الله عنایتنده وحضرت رسولك معجزاتی برکاتنده ایچنده اولان اکی دزداری طوپدن هلاك اولب وکفرهٔ ملاعین عاجز وفرومانده اولب هلاك اولمماغه راضی اولب مع ما فیها من الانفس والاموال سلطانه تسلیم اتدیلر سلطان بایزید خانوك اکنجی فتحی بودر سلطان مذکور همان ساعت قاضی ودزدار نصب ایدوب کلیسالرن مسجد وچاکلقلرن مناره ایدوب جمعه نمازن قلدی سلطان مذکور قلعه‌نوك خرابن عسکرنه امر ایدوب فی الحال تعمیر اندردکدن صکره کرك اولان

مصالحدن مستحفظلرن وساير آلاتن واسبابن مرتّب ومكمّل ايدوب
اموال غنايمدن مجلسنه بى نهايه انعام واحسان ايدوب مزبور رجبنوك
يكرمِ اكنجى كوننده شنبه كون اق كرمان ازرندن قالقوب كلوب كلى
قلعسى اوكندن كچدى اندن يوريوب طونه صوينى صارو صلتوق بابا
طوشندن كچوب سالماً وغانماً سنهٔ مذكور شعباننوك اواخرنده دولت
واقبال برله دار العزّ ادرنيه يتشوب سرايه كيروب عدل وداد اتمكه
مشغول اولدى

تمّت الكتاب بعون عنايت الملك الوهّاب

APPENDIX III

NESHRĪ'S CHRONOLOGICAL LIST

In these quotations from the two latest extant chronological lists are included all the passages whose parallels Neshrī seems to have borrowed from the very similar list which he used. The text is that of MS. Bağdad Köşkü 309, for 856, with the few variants of MS. Nur-i Osmaniye 3080 (N), for 858, given in brackets. The dates appended are the Hijra years indicated by the retrospective dates of the lists: e.g., for the first item quoted, the earlier list has '101 years ago', the later '103', indicating A.H. 755.

وکالی بُولی غازی مراد خانبك النده فتح اوللدن برو . . . [755]

وقاضی برهان الدّین برله یلدرم بایزید خان واقعه‌سندن برو قرق
دلمده . . . [799]

وسلطان بایزید خان وارب نکده حصارن فتح ایدب قرمان اوغلی محمّد
بکی وعلی بکی اسیر ایدب . . . [801]

وسلطان محمّد خانبك بکشهرن وحمید ولایتلرن وسیدی شهرن وأوقلق
حصارن وسعید ایلن فتح ایدب وارب قونیه شهرن حصار ایدب
وبغایت قَتِ سیل کلب چوق یرلری خراب ایدب وأورده‌یی سیل
الب سلطان محمّد خان قرمان اوغلیله صُلح ایدب . . . [818]

وجانیق ولایتلرن وقسطمونیّه‌نك بعضی ولایتلرن فتح ادلدن برو . . .
[819]

وسلطان محمّد خان طُون صُوین کَچُبْ افلاق ولایتلرن غارت ادلدن
وآتدن دُشلدن برو . . . [820]

وبروسه شهرنده وَرُوم ولایتلرنده قَتِ زلزله اولب یر دپرنلدن وبعضی
یرلری خراب أوللدن برو . . . [822]

وپیر عمر واقعه‌سندن وقره یوسف وفاتندن واوغلی اسکندر جلوسندن
وشاه رُخ کلب واسکندر قچب کلب تبریز تختنده پادشاه اوللدن برو
[823] وشاه رُخ جمیع ترکمان اوردسن غارت ادلدن برو . . .

. . . وَرُوم ایلنه یلدرم بایزید خان اوغلی مُصطفی بك پادشاه اوللدن
برو ومصر پادشاهی شیخی سلطان وفاتندن وتاتار بك جُلوسندن
[824] ومنتشا اوغلی الیاس بك وفاتندن . . .

[824] وتاتار بك واقعه‌سندن وبارس بك مصرده پادشاه اوللدن . . .

وسلطان مراد خان استنبول شهرنی حصار ادلدن وقرنداشی مُصطفی بك
ومخال اوغلی وتاج الدّین اوغلی واقعه‌لرندن برو ازنیق شهرنده . . .

[826]

[828] ووزیر حاجی عوض پاشا واقعه‌سندن برو . . .

ودزمه مصطفی کفه‌دن کلب سلطان مراد خان النده هلاك اوللدن
ومخال اوغلی وقاسم اوغلی وشا [شاه : N] ملك وروم ایلی بکلربك
[بکلرنك : N] واقعه‌لرندن وشام چریسی قبروزی فتح ادلدن . . .

[830]

ولاز اوغلی وفاتندن وولق اوغلی جُلوسندن وغازی سلطان مراد خان
کوکرجنلك حصارن حصار ادلدن برو وانکروس کلب وروم ایلی
چرسی وارب وانکروس قچب اسلام چرسی انکروسك صوکن غارت
ادلدن وکندز اوغلی واقعه‌سندن وبروسه شهرنده قتِ وبا واُولَتْ
دشلدن برو وسلطان مراد خان قرنداشی [قرنداشلری : N] وامیر
سُلیمان پادشاه اوغلی اورخانبك وامیر سید وابرهیم پاشا وحاجی
عوض وچراق بك وشیخ فخر الدّین افندی اوغلنلری ومولانا شمس
الدّین سلطان العلمآ فناری اوغلی علیهم الرحمةً واسعةً [رحمة الله
علیهم رحمة واسعة : N] وفاتلرندن برو وشام چرسی قره یلك اوزرنه

وارب رُوحا شهرن خراب ایدُبْ قره یلك اوغلی هابلی اسیر ادلدن
وقره یلك وارب شاه رُخی کترب قره یوسُف اوغلی اسکندر بك اوزرنه
کلب واسکندر قچب وشاه رُخ ترکمانلرك اوغلنلرن وقزلرن
وعورتلرن اسیر ایدب اوردُسن غارت ادلدن برو [و + :N] جمیع
عراق ولایتلرن خراب ادلدن وصکره قتِ قزلق وقحط واجلق دُشُبْ
چُوقلق خلق اول سببدن هلاك أوللدن برو وبعضیلری شامه وروسه
دوکللدن | وسلطان محمّد خان ولادتندن وسلانك سلطان غازی مراد
خان النده فتح ادلدن [ادللدن : N] برو وکمیلر کالی‌بُولی بغازن
دُتُبْ اسیر سلیمان بورغوزن حصار ایدُب چوق جنك وقتال اُولُب
صکره سلطان مراد خانله مُصالحه ایدب کمیلر کدن [کدلدن : N]
برو . . . [833]

وسلطان مراد خان حکمیله امیر سلیمان برغوزن خراب ادلدن برو . . .
[833]

ومصر سلطانی بارس بك حمید شهرنه وقره یُلك اوزرنه وارب صکره صلح
ایدب کدلدن وکنش دکلی دُوتلبْ بغایتْ قراکولق اولب یلدزلر
ظهوره کللدن برو . . . [834]

وسلطان غازی مراد خان وقرمان اوغلی عیسی بك وذو القدر اوغلی
سلیمان بك وقاضی برهان الدّین اوغلی زین العابدین قرمان اوغلی
ابرهیم بك اوزرنه وارب . . . وسلطان العلما محمّد شاه پاشا رحمة [sic]
الله رحمةً واسعةً وفاتندن برو وسلطان مراد خان قرمان اوغلی ابرهیم
بکله مُصالحه ادلدن وقرمان اوغلی عیسی بك واقعه‌سندن برو . . .
[839]

وسلطان مراد خان سمندره اوزرنه وارب فتح ادلدن وتمور خان اوغلی
شاه رُخ قره یوسُف اوغلی اسکندر اوزرنه کلب واسکندر قچب رُوسه

کلدن وشاه رُخ جمیع عراق ولایتلرن غارت وخراب ادلدن برو
وجهانشا وارب عراق ولایتلرنه پادشاه أوللدن وقره یلك اسکندر
النده هلاك أولُبْ واسکندر النجه حصارنده أوغلی وعَوْرتی النده
هلاك اوللدن برو ومصر شام چرسی رومه کلب اینق حسن حصارن
خراب ایدب ارزنجان وسیواس أوزرنه کلب صکره دُونُبْ شامه
کدلدن ومصر سلطانی بارس بك وفاتندن واوغلی جلوسندن وصُکره
چقمق امیرخور بارس بك اوغلن دتب مصر تختنده پادشاه اوللدن
برو[1] وسلطان مراد بل‌اغراط اوزرنه وارلدن برو . . . [842]

ومراد خان زماننده نوبری شهری وبعضی یرلر کافرلر ولایتلرندن رُوم
ایلنده شهاب الدّین پاشا النده فتح اوللدن برو وبعضی حصارلر أوج
بکی اسحاق بك النده فتح اوللدن برو . . . [844]

وامیر اخور مزید بك واقعه‌سندن برو وقرمان اوغلی ابرهیم بك اقشهری
وبکشهرن یقب غارت ادلدن برو . . . [845]

وسلطان مراد قرمان اوغلی ابرهیم بك اوزرنه وارب قرمان أُوغلی
ابرهیم بك قچب وسلطان مراد خان وسلطان علادین [علاء
الدّین : N] بك سلطان مراد خان اوغلی قونیه شهرن ولارنده شهرن
وولایتلرن خراب وغارت ادلدن برو وصکره سلطان مراد خان قرمان
اوغلی ابرهیم بکله مُصالحه ایدب کدلدن برو وسلطان مراد خان
اوغلی علادین [علاء الدّین : N] بك وفاتندن وفناری اوغلی یُوسف
بالی مرحوم و [ومرحوم : N] قاضی برهان الدّین اوغلی زین العابدین
وفاتلرندن برو وقرمان اوغلی ابرهیم بك کلب [قچب : N] کرمیان
ولایتلرن وبولاودین وقیرشهرن وبك بازارن وسفری حصاری

[1] N has lost (by haplography) the first five words of this paragraph. It also distributes the events between two years, those to this point being assigned to [841], and the last item only to [842].

وانكوريه ولايتن وعمر طاغن وقره حصار وكوتاهيّه شهرن وولايتلرن وبعضى حميد ايلى ولايتلرن غارت وخراب ادلدن برو . . .

[846]

وسلطان مراد خان اوغلى سلطان محمّد خان جلوسندن وسلطان مراد خان قرمان اوغلى ابرهيم بك اوزرنه وارب ويكى شهرده اوترب قرار ادلدن وقرهمان اوغلى ابرهيم بكله مصالحه ايدب . . . [847]

APPENDIX IV

STEMMA OF THE NESHRĪ MANUSCRIPTS

THE argument for the construction of the stemma at p. 41 runs as follows:

i. MSS. MnAFWPa fall into two groups, MnA and FWPa, for FWPa often have extra matter lacking in MnA (cf. *Ank*, apparatus to 543, 10; 550, 6; 572, 16; 592, 13; 596, 9), and FWPa have headings in Turkish where MnA have headings in Persian (422, 1; 424, 5; 428, 6; 430, 12). Since Mz represents an earlier recension of the text (Ch. IV), it provides a touchstone for deciding which group preserves the original tradition for each criterion: comparison shows that the extra passages in FWPa are additions (for they are lacking also in Mz) and that the Persian headings of MnA are an aberration (for Mz has these headings in Turkish). Hence the two groups are independent:

Archetype

MnA FWPa

ii. In the group MnA: Mn has a peculiar error (an omission) at 520, 13, against A and FWPa; A has extensive additions (at 546, 7; 610, 12; 636, 10; 664, 7, &c.) against Mn and FWPa. Hence Mn and A derive independently from a common exemplar, the hyparchetype β.

iii. In the group FWPa: F and W share peculiar errors at 556, 17 (omission by haplography) and 422, 6, against Pa and MnA; Pa has an addition at 666, 8, against MnA and FW. Hence FW and Pa derive independently from a hyparchetype γ.

iv. In the sub-group FW: F has peculiar errors at 482, 5; 562, 16; 658, 1 (additions) and 484, 9; 602, 6 (omissions), against MnA and WPa; W has peculiar errors at 448, 6; 538, 6; 624, 15, against MnA and FPa. Hence they derive from a common exemplar δ.

v. The variants of V are given only to *Ank* 146 and from *Ank* 686 onwards, but they are sufficient to show that V belongs to the group γ (cf. 710, 10 and 11; 718, 1) and within it to the sub-group δ (710, 15; 772, 2), where it stands closest to F (712, 1; 720, 2; 776, 2). However, as V has additions of its own (784, 16; 788, 1; 790, 2; 794, 5), and sometimes stands against F with the other members of group γ (PaW, cf. 810, 7; 816, 7), V and F must derive from a common exemplar ϵ.

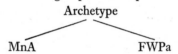

APPENDIX V

AUTOBIOGRAPHICAL REFERENCES IN MS Pb

Fol. 81ᵛ, 1–16:

اولوقت فقیر الاشهر نواحی‌سنده دلولر نام قریه‌ده خطیب اولوب
استانبوله وارمشدم امام علی قاضیعسکر وعلی پاشا وزیر اعظم وداود
پاشا وزیر اولدی فی اوایل آخری جمادین هجره‌تك سـ ٨٩٧/٢٣ ـنه‌سنده
شعبانده شاه چلبی واقعه‌یه اوغرایوب وهم طاعون اولدی التی آی
تمام بز فقیر استانبولدن قالقوب سیاحتله ازمیره کلدوکم غرّهٔ رجب
ایدی اتّفاق قُورت قاضی ایدی شعبان آینده طاعون بلورب صوفی الیاس
فوت اولدی اندن کاتب اولوب ذی الحجّه اوایلنده استانبوله واروب
کتابت برآتن الدم هجره‌تلـ ٨٩٨/٢٢ ـك تاریخ سنه‌سنده واقع اولمشدر اندن
بر یلدن صکره تاهّل ایتدوکم ماه محرم ایدی سـ ٨٩٩/٢١ ـنه هجرتندن
ایدی اندن صکره بر بچق سنه هجره‌تلـ ٩٠١/١٩ ـك سنه ییلك ایچنده دولتلو
شوکتلو خنکار آناطولی بکلربکسی احمد پاشایه تفتیش عامّه ویریلوب
آیدین ایلنه وازمیره کلدوکی جماذی الآخر آیی ایدی اندن ینه
کوتاهیّه‌یه واروب اوتوررکن هجرتك سـ ٩٠٢/١٨ ـنه‌سنده یلك رمضانی
غره‌سنده احمد پاشایی بکلربکی‌لکدن وزارته دعوت ایدوب اناطولی
بکلربکیسی سنان پاشا اولدی اولوقت کلیبولی بکیدی فقیر دخی اولحینده
حصار علایّه‌ده امام اولمشدم فی اوایل ذی القعده محمّد چلبی قاضی
اولدی اندن هجرتلـ ٩٠٣/١٧ ـك سنه اولیجق . . .

Fol. 82r, 14–21:

فقیر ذی القعده آینده ادرنیه واروب جنید بك عمارتن آلوب كلدم
پس هجره‌تك سنه‌سنده [sic] واقعدر اندن خنكار كچوب قدم قدم
كیدوب اضحیه بیرامنی یكی‌شهرده ایدوب قالقوب ذی الحجه‌نك
یكرمی‌سنده ابراهیم پاشا فوت اولوب احمد پاشا وزیر اعظم اولدی
اینه‌بختی اوزرینه دوشب حق تعالینك فضلی برله اینه‌بختی فتح
اولندی هجره‌تلـــك ٩٠٥ ١٥ تاریخنده محرّم آیی ایچنده اندن كلوب ادرنه‌ده
اوتوردی اندن استانبوله كلوب علی پاشایه موره سنجاغن ویروب فایق
پاشا مرحوم اولدی

Fol. 82v, 2–5, 10–13, 16, 19–23, 83r, 1–5:

خنكار . . . قالقوب دولتله استانبوله كلیجك امام علیٔ قاضیعسكرلكدن
معزول ایدوب مؤیّدزاده كلوب اوتوردی آخر ربیعینده برآت تربداری
اندن آلدم امّا ربیع الاوّل آینده مدلّلو اوزرینه كافر دوشوب كمال
رئیس كلوب ازمیر لیمانته قاچوب كردی اوتوردی . . .

اندن خنكار تیره سنجاغی بكی یعقوب اغایه امر ایدوب كلوب
حصارك خراب اولان یرین پابدروب ایچنه عزب قویوب معمور ایتدیلر
اندن مذكور ییلك ایچنده ذی القعده آینده قلعهٔ علائیّه‌یه امام اولوب
. . . اسكدارده آلمشدم برآتی فقیر ذی القعده آینده ایدی . . . اندن
وفات عبد الرّحمان بن خاص بكی فقیر امام ایدم قلعده شعبان آینده
ایدی هجرتلـــك ٩٠١ ١٠ [sic] سنه‌سنده اندن هجره‌تك ســـنه ٩١١ قلعدن
اینوب ربیع الآخر آینك اون طقوزنجی كونی پنچشنبه كیجه‌سی
محمّدك ممی حوجه دنیایه كلوب ذی الحجّه‌ده استانبوله واروب امام
محمود قاضیعسكر اولوب . . . (83r) كچوچك داد [sic] پاشا وزیری [sic]
ایدی فوت اولدی هجره‌تلـــك ٩١١ ٠٠٩ سنه‌سنده ذی الحجّه‌سنده كاتب

وخطیب اولدم قوز اغاجه امّا صاصه بك ایل یزمغه کلدوکی مذکور یلك شعبان آینده ایدی . . . وداخی سلطان محمود قسطمونیه‌دن کلوب معنیساده بك اولدوغی سببدن خوجه‌سی ایوکلو خیر الدّین ازمیره قاضی اولدی . . .

Fol. 84ᵛ, 4–5, 8–10, 14–16:

مبارك رمضانك آینده جمیعی اهل برآت تجدید برآت ایتدیلر مبارك رمضان آخرنده فقیرك براتی تجدید اولدی . . . اندن قورقود بك ازمیردن معنیسایه کلمشدی ذی القعده آینده الغار ایدوب دولتلو خنکار معنیسایه کلوب . . . بر ایکی هفته خنکار اوتوروب دولتله کیدیجك قورقود بکك نقدر اتباعی وار ایسه اوّل وآخر بورسیه سورمکه قبوجی باشی سنان بك کلوب سوردلر

Fol. 87ᵛ, 3–8:

ولطفی افندی‌یه دربولس قاضیلغن ویردوکی شوّال آینده ایدی هجره‌تلك ۹۲۲ سنه‌سنده اندن مکّه بکنه وغزّایه ومصره آدملر پراکنده اولنوب وقورد رئیس اوغلی ازمیره وسلیمان رئیس دخی اسکندریّیه کلدوکی ذی القعده آینده ایدی معنیسا عمر چلبی‌یه وتیره زیرك‌زاده‌نك کیچی‌سنه ویرلدی سیدی چلبی ثمانیه مدرّسی اولدی وبعده سنان پاشا خنکار اوکنجه غزایه واروب . . .

INDEX

This index ignores references to persons and places mentioned only in quotations and in discussions of the content of historical texts

PRINTED IN GREAT BRITAIN
AT THE UNIVERSITY PRESS, OXFORD
BY VIVIAN RIDLER
PRINTER TO THE UNIVERSITY